COLLECTOR'S GUIDE TO

T.S.&T.
Taylor Smith Taylor
"PREMIER POTTERS OF AMERICA"

Lu-RAY

PASTELS
U. S. A.

FEATURING: Conversation
Pebbleford
Vistosa & more

Bill & Kathy Meehan

COLLECTOR BOOKS
A Division of Schroeder Publishing Co., Inc.

The current values in this book should be used only as a guide. They are not intended to set prices, which vary from one section of the country to another. Auction prices, as well as dealer prices, vary greatly and are affected by condition as well as demand. Neither the Authors nor the Publisher assume responsibility for any losses that might be incurred as a result of consulting this guide.

Searching For A Publisher?

We are always looking for knowledgeable people considered to be experts within their fields. If you feel that there is a need for a book on your collectible subject and have a large comprehensive collection, contact us.

COLLECTOR BOOKS
P.O. Box 3009
Paducah, Kentucky 42002-3009

BOOK DESIGN BY SHERRY KRAUS
COVER DESIGN BY BETH SUMMERS
PHOTOGRAPHY BY TED BARRON & BILL MEEHAN

Additional copies of this book may be ordered from:

COLLECTOR BOOKS
P.O. Box 3009
Paducah, Kentucky 42002-3009
or
Bill & Kathy Meehan
P.O. Box 2054
Haddonfield, NJ 08033

@ $18.95. Add $2.00 for postage and handling.

DEDICATION

For our daughter

LILY

COLLECTING T.S.& T.

Left to right: Pebbleford sauceboat, Lu-Ray relish dish, "Silhouette" on Laurel saucer, Pebbleford handled covered sugar, Lu-Ray cream soup cup and saucer, Vistosa water jug, Lu-Ray chop plate, Empire teapot, Conversation coffee server, Lu-Ray coaster, Lu-Ray bud vase, Lu-Ray flower vase.

ACKNOWLEDGMENTS

No book of this type can be written without the enthusiastic assistance of many people. We would like to thank the following people who helped us with our research, photography, and illustrations:

Wilma Dailey Eardley, former T.S.&T. inventory manager, provided us with information about T.S.&T. and its home, Chester, West Virginia.

William L. Smith, III, former T.S.&T executive, gave us information about Lu-Ray Pastels.

John Lesser of John Lesser & Associates, Williamstown, NJ, gave us valuble photography advice, photographic criticism, and helped us with trouble shooting.

Richard Winther and Diane Misciagno suggested techniques for photographing dinnerware.

Debbie Dornan provided information about her grandfather, T.S.&T. salesman A. H. Dornan.

Betty Llalas, collector, provided information about unusual pieces in the Lu-Ray Pastels line.

Thelma Steiff, former T.S.&T. employee, shared information about her career at T.S.&T.

Our special thanks to the following individuals without whom this book could not have been written:

Ed Stump, owner, Raccoon's Tale Antiques, Mullica Hill, NJ, introduced us to other collectors willing to help with this book and helped locate hard to find T.S.&T. lines.

Donald Doctorow, publisher of the industry magazine *China, Glass & Tableware*, Clifton, NJ, kindly allowed us free use of his magazine's archives. He shared his knowledge of the pottery industry and permitted us to quote from period articles about T.S.&T. and its products.

Juanita Cline, former T.S.&T. bookeeper, generously shared recollections of her career at T.S.&T., gave us use of her notes, papers, and photos, and introduced us to other former T.S.&T. employees.

Ed Nenstiel, collector and promoter of interest in Lu-Ray Pastels, whose groundbreaking research was the nucleus of our knowledge of Lu-Ray Pastels and T.S.&T.

Our good friend, artist Erich Lorenz v. Benndorff, for the original illustrations created expressly for this book.

Our new friends, collectors Bob Brown and Tim Novak, generously invited us to photograph their collection of T.S.&T. products, the largest known to the authors, and volunteered their home for our studio. In addition they solicited information from other collectors to help make this book as complete as possible.

Lisa Stroup, Sherry Kraus, and Beth Summers of Collector Books, whose creativity and belief in the project truly brought it to life.

Finally, we thank our good friend Ted Barron. Ted doesn't collect anything, but has been a good sport about our collecting interests and the projects they have generated for more than twenty-three years. An accomplished engineer, Ted designed and built the equipment needed for the photography for this book and took all of the photographs, a process that occupied most weekends for several months. Having Ted in our collection of friends makes us very fortunate collectors.

CONTENTS

Introduction – A Drive in the Country...6

PART I — LU-RAY PASTELS

CHAPTER 1 – For Modern Charming Tables...7
         The History of Lu-Ray Pastels
         1938 to 1961
CHAPTER 2 – Set Your Table with Jewels 17
         A Catalog of Lu-Ray Pastels
CHAPTER 3 – Collecting Lu-Ray Pastels 33

PART II — OTHER LINES BY THE TAYLOR, SMITH & TAYLOR CO. (T.S.& T.)

CHAPTER 4 – The Griffin...37
         T.S.&T. from 1900 to 1930
CHAPTER 5 – Premier Potters of America..47
         1930 to 1955
CHAPTER 6 – Vistosa 73
         1938 to circa 1942
CHAPTER 7 – Coral-Craft...83
         1939
CHAPTER 8 – Conversation 84
         Designed by Walter Dorwin Teague
         1950 to 1954
CHAPTER 9 – America's Most Versatile Dinnerware....................................91
         Versatile
         1952 to circa 1965
CHAPTER 10 – Pebbleford, for Round-the-Clock Modern Living...............101
         1952 to circa 1960
CHAPTER 11 – In the Continental Tradition 114
         Chateau Buffet and Oven-Serve
         1956 to circa 1965
CHAPTER 12 – American Fine China...117
         Taylorton
         1958 to circa 1965
CHAPTER 13 – Ever Yours 123
         1958 to circa 1965
CHAPTER 14 – Classic...130
         1960 to 1972
CHAPTER 15 – Ironstone 132
         Taylorstone, Taylor Ironstone and Related Lines
         1963 to 1981
CHAPTER 16 – The Ceramic Products Division of Anchor Hocking Corporation........137
         1972 to 1981
Value Guide 140
Bibliography 157

INTRODUCTION

A DRIVE IN THE COUNTRY

Our first look at Lu-Ray Pastels came during the summer of 1990. After a wonderful Sunday brunch, we were exploring the beautiful winding back roads of Bucks County, Pennsylvania, and discovered an antique shop called Oma's Attic. Despite the name, the shop shared space with farm equipment in a barn.

Right inside the door was a table set with a complete, 16-piece, mint-condition set of Lu-Ray in the original four colors. The farmer's wife had arranged the four place settings on a table, as if for a luncheon, and it triggered memories of having seen pastel dinnerware before, perhaps as a child. The set was reasonably priced and we decided to buy it.

As we found more items to add to our set, we became increasingly interested in Lu-Ray, and wanted to learn all we could about it. We had bought some Collector Books on other American dinnerware lines but were unable to find one covering Lu-Ray Pastels in depth.

We discovered that Collector Books did not have a Lu-Ray book in its catalog. We called editor Lisa Stroup at Collector Books and learned that no Lu-Ray book was planned. She half-jokingly said, "Would you like to write one?" We thought it over and decided to give it a try.

As we researched the Lu-Ray Pastels line and its manufacturer, The Taylor, Smith and Taylor Company, we realized that to tell Lu-Ray's story in context we would need to cover other lines. We soon expanded our study to cover all known T.S.&T. products. Some of these, such as Vistosa, Coral-Craft, Conversation, and Pebbleford are already widely collected, while many others are less popular.

We have tried to answer all the questions of when, where, who, why, and how T.S.&T.'s dinnerware lines were made. Unfortunately, as with other former manufacturers, whatever records the pottery might have kept on their wares have been lost or destroyed, making some of these questions difficult or impossible to answer.

While this book is as complete as we could make it today, we are still interested in gathering more information about T.S.&T. and its products for future editions. We would like to hear from others who have information to share.

We hope you enjoy our book as much as we've enjoyed putting it together for you.

Bill & Kathy Meehan

CHAPTER 1

FOR MODERN CHARMING TABLES

The History of Lu-Ray Pastels
1938 to 1961

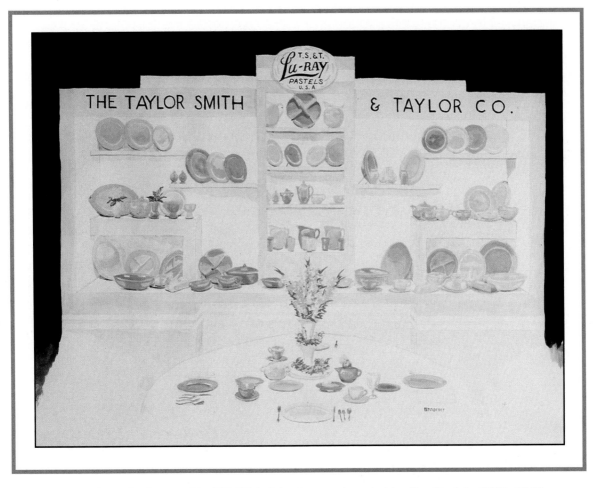

Trade show display used by T.S.&T. to introduce and market Lu-Ray Pastels, 1938–1942.
Original art by Erich Lorenz v. Benndorff from period photographs.

The suspense was building. The industry was abuzz with excitement. In the summer of 1938, The Taylor, Smith & Taylor Company of Chester, West Virginia, was about to take a bold marketing step with the introduction of their innovative Lu-Ray Pastels dinnerware line.

Famous for creating an aura of anticipation before introducing a new line, T.S.& T. took out a full page ad in the June 1938 issue of *China, Glass & Lamps* telling buyers to, "Plan now to see our first showing of smart new lines at the New York China Glass and Housewares Show. . ." After T.S.&T's introduction of Vistosa in January, the industry was especially interested in seeing what they had in store for the July show.

And no one was disappointed. What they found was a specially built Art Deco breakfront and table bursting with the new Lu-Ray colors and shapes. Their advertisement that August proclaimed, "T.S.&T. leads in presenting pastels." And lead the market they did!

The 1930s: A Festival of Brightly-Colored Dinnerware

Since 1930 when the J.A. Bauer Pottery Company of California introduced their Mexican-influenced, primary-colored dinnerware, American kitchen tables had been ablaze with hot reds, yellows, greens, and blues. Other companies quickly began to market their own brightly-colored dinnerware. Companies such as Paden City, Edwin M. Knowles, Franciscan, Vernon Kilns, and the Metlox Poppy Trail Manufacturing Company, all threw their hats into the ring with a flare before the end of the 1930s.

Of course, the most successful of the primary-colored dinnerware patterns was the Homer Laughlin China Company's Fiesta which made its debut in January of 1936. Fiesta is extremely popular with collectors today. On February 28, 1986, Homer Laughlin reintroduced its line of Fiesta with updated colors which to date is still in production.

T.S.&T. had also joined the Art Deco "festive" dinnerware movement through the introduction of their brightly-colored Vistosa pattern in January 1938.

The Contrast of Soft Pastel Hues

It was with Lu-Ray Pastels that T.S.&T. became a trend setter. The company recognized that not all American women fancied their meat loaf and mashed potatoes on neon-colored dinner plates. They realized that many women wanted to be fashionable without being flashy. They were excited to discover an unexplored niche in the dinnerware market and developed the softly-colored Lu-Ray Pastels line that would lead their company's sales for more than 20 years.

Lu-Ray is Introduced

Lu-Ray was first seen at the New York China, Glass and Housewares Show held at the Hotel Pennsylvania, July 10 through July 16, 1938. It was very well received. Taylor, Smith & Taylor's August 1938 ad copy explains the motivation behind Lu-Ray's development. "Completing the color cycle in modern dinnerware, we offer delightfully delicate pastels on the new Lu-Ray shape. . . .This line meets the demand for subtle colors and is a worthy companion for our more vivid Vistosa Pottery."

The Name Lu-Ray

There has been a mystery surrounding the name Lu-Ray which has finally been resolved. For many years, collectors have been guessing about the name's origins. But, a recent conversation with William L. "Bill" Smith III, former T.S.&.T. vice president and sales manager and the son and great-nephew of T.S.&.T's founders, cleared up the mystery. Lu-Ray was named for the beautiful Luray Caverns of Virginia.

"One of the company's leading salesmen at the time had just been to the Luray Caverns and had seen the colors," said Smith. He confirmed that the name was suggested by the salesman who had been inspired by a trip to the caverns.

Juanita Cline, T.S.&.T.'s bookkeeper, remembered the salesman. "It was Mr. A. H. Dornan, our top salesman, who had the East as his territory, who named Lu-Ray. He used to tease us and remind us that he came up with the name whenever he visited the office."

December 1938 ad for Lu-Ray Pastels.

Luray Caverns brochure, circa 1935.

Lu-Ray Colors

When introduced, Lu-Ray was available in four soft Easter-egg colors named Windsor Blue, Surf Green, Persian Cream, and Sharon Pink. The Persian Cream is actually more of a pale yellow than a cream. The colors are delicate foils to the cobalt blues, bright greens, sunny yellows, and hot reds so popular in the primary-colored lines.

In 1949, a fifth color was added called Chatham Gray. Although the gray blended beautifully with the other four shades, it was never as popular. Due to its short production run, today's collectors have a difficult time finding Chatham Gray pieces and often must pay a higher price when they do find a piece.

Lu-Ray Pastels brochure. This is the third known edition, believed to have been issued in 1948.

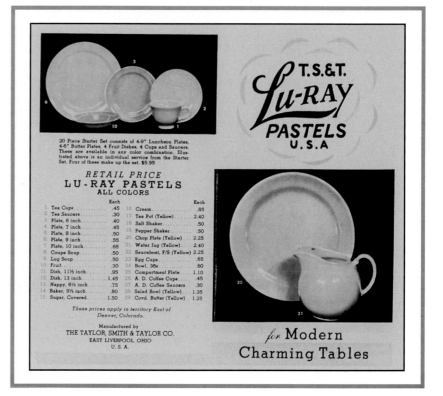

The first advertisement for Lu-Ray published in trade journals in August 1938.
This was the only Lu-Ray trade advertisement to be printed in color.

Spring Brides

From the beginning, Lu-Ray was heavily promoted in the spring as young brides chose colors and patterns for their new lives. In January 1939 an ad in *China, Glass and Lamps* told retailers, "If you display Lu-Ray as an Easter Special in a breakfast set, you will go to town."

A March 1939 Lu-Ray ad copy told housewives, "You can bring a breath of spring right into your dining room these days by setting your table with lovely Lu-Ray. Colors inspired by the beautiful pastel tints of spring flowers. . . and strictly modern shapes which in themselves are decorative without added design or floral. Every piece needed for complete breakfast, luncheon, or dinner service is available in sets or your own selection from open stock. Be sure to see Lu-Ray. You'll be wild about its festive springtime beauty."

According to *China, Glass & Lamps*, Gimbels Department Store in Manhattan featured Lu-Ray at its spring 1939 sale. "Taylor, Smith & Taylor's 'Lu-Ray' pastel dinnerware was given a generous display space near the elevators, topped by a huge placard which advised customers 'Give your table a beauty treatment.'" Each year through 1942, new items were added early in the year in time for spring sales.

Lu-Ray Pastels from left: individual covered sugar, individual cream, relish dish, after-dinner coffee pot, bud vase, and fruit juice jug.

Lu-Ray Pastels from left: double egg cup, compartment plate, bud vase, after-dinner coffee pot, covered butter, and fruit juice jug.

Lu-Ray Shapes

Upon Lu-Ray's introduction, Taylor, Smith & Taylor referred to the "new Lu-Ray shape." In fact, Lu-Ray shapes are mostly reincarnations of pieces from Taylor, Smith & Taylor's Laurel and Empire lines. Laurel was introduced in early 1933 and Empire in 1936. (Please see Chapter 5 for more information about Laurel and Empire.)

For the most part Lu-Ray hollowware is all Empire. An exception is the cream soup which is the Laurel shape. The flatware is all Laurel. Among the pieces believed to be designed specifically for the Lu-Ray line were the tea cup, the tea saucer, the after-dinner cup and the after-dinner saucer. (Please see Chapter 2 for more detailed information about specific pieces in the line.)

September 1938 advertisement copy described the Lu-Ray shape as "Graceful, streamlined. . . the thin body feeling of the finest. . . and pastel colors that are uniform to the point of winning, in any side by side comparison. . . that's what fascinates style-conscious women. They realize that here at last is just what they need to complete the ensemble of perfectly modern service."

Sweet Success

As predicted, Lu-Ray did become wildly successful and inspired other companies to come out with soft, pastel patterns. Lu-Ray was Taylor, Smith & Taylor's biggest selling line. By the late 1940s, a billboard-sized sign on the side of The Taylor, Smith & Taylor Company factory read, "Lu-Ray Pastel Dinnerware" on one side and "The Taylor, Smith & Taylor Company" on the other side giving equal prominence to their best-selling line.

The Taylor, Smith & Taylor Company pottery in July, 1953.

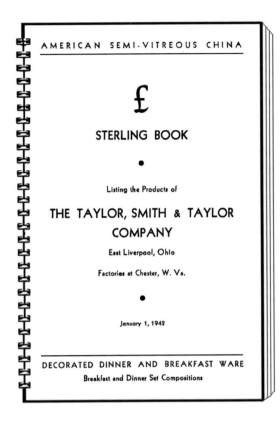

AMERICAN SEMI-VITREOUS CHINA

£

STERLING BOOK

•

Listing the Products of

THE TAYLOR, SMITH & TAYLOR
COMPANY

East Liverpool, Ohio

Factories at Chester, W. Va.

•

January 1, 1942

DECORATED DINNER AND BREAKFAST WARE
Breakfast and Dinner Set Compositions

January 1, 1942, edition of T.S.&T's "Pound Sterling Book." This edition was used to price T.S.&T. products until the company was bought by Anchor Hocking. All clerks had their own copy.

The $8.00 per pound sterling list was used to price Lu-Ray Pastels and some later lines.

The Taylor, Smith & Taylor Co.
"Premier Potters of America
EAST LIVERPOOL, OHIO

Composition of sets listed on LU-RAY order blanks is as follows:

No. 154   20 Pc. Set

4 Teas
4 Plates, 6 in.
4 Plates, 9 in.
4 Fruits, 5 in.

No. 267   32 Pc. Set

6 Teas
6 Plates, 6 in
6 Plates, 9 in.
6 Fruits, 5 in.
1 Dish, 11½ in.
1 Nappy, 8½ in.

No. 327   35 Pc. Set

6 Teas
6 Plates, 6 in
6 Plates, 9 in.
6 Fruits, 5 in.
1 Dish, 11½ in.
1 Nappy, 8½ in.
1 Sugar, Cov'd.
1 Creamer

No. 416   45 Pc. Set

8 Teas
8 Plates, 6 in.
8 Plates, 9 in.
8 Onion Soups
1 Dish, 13 in
1 Nappy, 8½ in.
1 Sugar, Cov'd.
1 Creamer

No. 523A   53 Pc. Set

8 Teas
8 Plates, 6 in.
8 Plates, 10 in.
8 Coupe Soups
8 Fruits, 5 in.
1 Dish, 13 in.
1 Nappy, 8½ in.
1 Sugar, Cov'd.
1 Creamer

Unless otherwise directed all sets will be made up of Assorted Colors

The Taylor, Smith & Taylor list of items in Lu-Ray sets. Of five different sets, only one, the 53 piece set, used 10" plates. The "onion soups" are lug soups. Sets were made up of assorted colors.

CHAPTER 2

SET YOUR TABLE WITH JEWELS

A Catalog of Lu-Ray Pastels

When Lu-Ray was introduced in 1938, the line consisted of 29 different pieces and was available in four colors — Windsor Blue, Surf Green, Persian Cream, and Sharon Pink. The items in the original line were:

Teacup	Pickle
Tea saucer	Sugar, covered
Plate, 6"	Cream
Plate, 7"	Casserole
Plate, 8"	Teapot "flat spout"
Plate, 9"	Salt Shaker
Plate, 10"	Pepper Shaker
Coupe Soup	Chop Plate, 15"
Lug Soup	Water Jug "footed"
Fruit, 5"	Cream Soup Cup
Dish, 11½"	Cream Soup Saucer
Dish, 13"	Sauceboat, fixed stand
Nappy, 8½"	Cake Plate
Baker, 9½"	Bowl, 36s
Sauceboat	

Also introduced in July 1938, "On the Lu-Ray blue, the Fifth Avenue pattern, a highly stylized flower and jar pattern against a checkerboard square, done in blue, green, and yellow." This line does not appear to have been successful. So far, no examples have been reported. However the line has been documented in trade magazine advertisements.

In January 1939 T.S.&T. made the first additions to the Lu-Ray line with the following items:

Flower Vase "epergne"	After-Dinner Coffee "chocolate" Saucers
Four-Part Relish	Individual "chocolate" Covered Sugar
After-Dinner Coffee "chocolate" Pot	Individual "chocolate" Cream
After-Dinner Coffee "chocolate" Cups	Double Egg Cups

This first, straight-sided version of the after-dinner coffee pot, cups, saucers, cream, and sugar is often referred to as the "chocolate set" by collectors. The next additions were in July 1939, when the bud urn and bud vase were added.

In January 1940, the muffin cover was introduced. Also in 1940, after only one year in production, the line's original, straight-sided after-dinner coffee set was replaced by an Empire-shape after-dinner coffee set including pot, cups, saucers, and individual cream and sugar. This explains the rarity of the so-called "chocolate set."

In January of 1941, additions included:

Mixing Bowl, 10¼"	Fruit Juice Jug
Mixing Bowl, 8¾"	Fruit Juice Tumbler
Mixing Bowl, 7"	Salad Bowl
Mixing Bowl, 5½"	Compartment Plate
Covered Butter	

Trade show photographs from the January 1941 New York Show revealed for the first time the curved-spout teapot which replaced the original, flat-spout type.

In September 1941, the first Lu-Ray sales brochure was issued, illustrating a total of 49 items and providing their retail prices. By this time, the water jug had lost its foot and the angle of its ice guard was reduced.

"Several new items in the much liked Lu-Ray Pastels, among them a coaster or ashtray with an etched design on the bottom and a ten-ounce tumbler" were added to the line in January 1942, according to *China, Glass & Tableware*. The small, etched dishes, called "nut dishes" by some collectors, are identified by T.S.&T. in their second Lu-Ray brochure as coasters.

The War Years

World War II had begun the previous month and these were to be the last items added to the Lu-Ray line. The War Production Board declared dinnerware a necessary consumer product, so production continued at T.S.&T. during the war. But, no new pieces or lines were introduced.

Many of T.S.&T.'s employees were away from their jobs while they served their country overseas, so some retired employees returned to work at the plant to replace the servicemen. In the trade journals, ads for new dinnerware lines were replaced by lists of killed and wounded men from the dinnerware industry.

Changing Times

The first post-war Lu-Ray price list was published in the *Crockery & Glass Journal* for March 1947. The line had been cut back to 29 pieces. This type of reduction, also seen in other dinnerware lines, was a reflection of changing tastes and lifestyles among the American middle class. Before the war, some middle and upper class American families had been able to afford a cook or day maid who prepared dinner and served it in the dining room. As wages rose, most families were no longer able to afford servants and began to serve themselves. As a result, dinnerware took on a more casual style.

Discontinued from the Lu-Ray Pastels line after the war were:

Sauceboat	Bud Vase
Pickle	Bud Urn
Casserole	Muffin Cover
Cream Soup Cup	Mixing Bowl, 10¾"
Cream Soup Saucer	Mixing Bowl, 8¾"
Cake Plate	Mixing Bowl, 7"
Flower Vase "epergne"	Mixing Bowl, 5½"
Relish Dish	Fruit Juice Jug
After-dinner Coffee Pot	Fruit Juice Tumbler
Individual Covered Sugar	Coaster
Individual Cream	Tumbler

Judging from the backstamps of surviving examples, many of these items were discontinued before 1947, but some remained in inventory in T.S.&T.'s warehouse. An internal company note dated March 20, 1947, shows the following discontinued items could still be purchased. The note reads, "Pickles at sixty cents each or $7.20 per dozen, fruit juice tumblers at twenty-five cents each or $3.00 per dozen and after-dinner coffee pots at $19.80 per dozen."

Introducing Chatham Gray

In 1948 a new Lu-Ray brochure was printed with the same items as the 1947 price list, but prices were higher. Also, some of the serving pieces were now available only in yellow which was the most popular color at the time.

Internal T.S.& T. memos from Sales Manager Lester C. Wittenberg dated May 1949, discussed which items would continue to be made only in yellow and the addition of a new color, Chatham Gray. The memos indicate that after May 1949, the water jug, fixed stand sauceboat, chop plate, teapot, and salad bowl would only be made in Persian Cream or yellow.

Trade journal ads for June of that year announced "Lu-Ray Pastels, The Outstanding Pastel Line on the Market Since 1938" was to be offered in "Five Lovely Colors including 'Chatham Gray.'"

In July a line decorated with six bands of platinum on Chatham Gray Lu-Ray was introduced, but was unsuccessful. Chatham Gray seems to have been discontinued after 1952.

Many popular new lines were introduced by T.S.&T. throughout the 1950s, but Lu-Ray continued to be the company's best selling line. It was finally discontinued in 1961, although some of the plates stocked in T.S.&T.'s warehouse were used for calendar plates into 1962. Other T.S.&T. shapes would be dipped in its colors and the original concept of a solid color, pastel dinnerware would become the inspiration for other T.S.&T. lines.

Lu-Ray plates. 10" $13.00–18.00,
9" $8.00–12.00, 8" $12.00–18.00,
7" $8.00–12.00, and 6" $3.00–5.00.

Compartment plate in Windsor Blue,
$18.00–25.00.

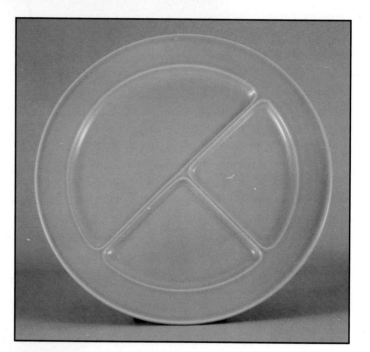

Large and small in the Lu-Ray line.
Chop plate $20.00–30.00,
coaster $60.00–75.00.

*Serving dishes in Lu-Ray.
Pickle $20.00–28.00,
11" dish $11.00–15.00,
13" dish $13.00–18.00.*

*The back of the 11"
and 13" Lu-Ray dish-
es. The one on the
left has a foot, the
one on the right does
not. These, along
with the bakers in the
Lu-Ray line, were
made with and with-
out feet. The pres-
ence or absence of a
foot has no special
significance.*

*Lu-Ray compartment plate
$18.00–25.00.*

*Sharon Pink Lu-Ray
cake plate $55.00–75.00.*

*Set of coasters in
Lu-Ray Pastels
$60.00–75.00 ea.*

*Sharon Pink Lu-Ray coaster
$60.00–75.00.*

Lu-Ray 1962, 9" calendar plate $35.00–50.00.

*Bowls in Lu-Ray.
From left: lug soup $15.00–22.00,
36s $25.00–40.00,
coupe soup $10.00–15.00,
cream soup cup and
saucer $68.00–85.00,
fruit $4.00–6.00.*

*Lu-Ray Serving Bowls.
Left to right: nappy $10.00–15.00, baker $13.00–18.00, salad bowl $38.00–55.00.*

*Lu-Ray Salad bowl
in Persian Cream
$38.00–55.00.*

*Lu-Ray nappy in Surf Green
$10.00–15.00.*

*36s bowl in Lu-Ray Pastels
$25.00–40.00.*

Cream soup cups and saucers in Lu-Ray Pastels $68.00–85.00 ea.

*Chatham Gray lug soup
$25.00–35.00.*

Covered casseroles in Lu-Ray Pastels. The Surf Green example on the left has a non-standard bronze band decorating the edge of the casserole bottom and its cover $60.00–80.00 ea.

Windsor Blue baker in Lu-Ray $13.00–18.00.

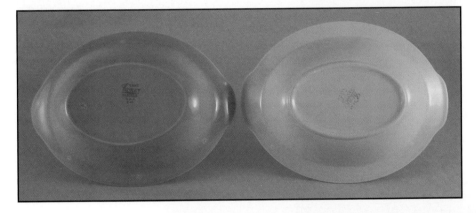

Lu-Ray bakers. Left does not have foot, right does. Some molds omitted the foot. $13.00–18.00 ea.

Lu-Ray water jugs. The original, footed design on the left $50.00–70.00, was replaced by the model on the right. $40.00–60.00.

*Nest of mixing bowls in
Lu-Ray Pastels
$290.00–380.00.*

*Lu-Ray mixing bowl set.
Left to right:
5½" $75.00–100.00,
7" $70.00–90.00,
8¾" $70.00–90.00,
10¼" $75.00–100.00.
Bowls are in each of the
original Lu-Ray colors.*

*Lu-Ray Pastels
fruit juice tumblers $30.00–40.00 ea.,
and fruit juice jug $100.00–130.00.*

*Lu-Ray Pastels
fruit juice tumblers (front)
$30.00–40.00,
and tumblers $45.00–60.00.*

*Empire shape Lu-Ray after-dinner
coffee pot introduced in 1940,
$125.00–150.00.*

*Original type of Lu-Ray
after-dinner coffee pot $350.00–375.00.
These were offered only during 1939.*

*Lu-Ray after-dinner coffee pots.
On the left is the original design,
called by some collectors the
"chocolate pot" $350.00–375.00.
The Empire shape that
replaced it is on the right.*

*Lu-Ray teapots $45.00–60.00 ea., teacups $7.00–10.00 ea., saucers $2.00–3.00 ea.,
in the original four colors.*

*"Flat spout " and "curved spout" Lu-Ray teapots. The angle of the handles is also different.
The curved spout type, $45.00–60.00 replaced the flat spout variety $60.00–75.00.*

*The original design for the Empire and Lu-Ray teapots, called "flat spout" by collectors. The
decaled versions are easier to find than Lu-Ray $60.00–75.00.*

*Chatham Gray Lu-Ray teacup
and saucer $20.00–24.00,
and the Lu-Ray shape after-
dinner coffee cup and saucer
$36.00–45.00. These cups and
saucers were designed specifically for Lu-Ray.*

Left: Original design of the after-dinner coffee cup and saucer $70.00–95.00, compared with the later version on the right $22.00–32.00.

Sharon Pink Lu-Ray teacup $7.00–10.00, on the right and an Empire teacup $2.00, on the left. The Lu-Ray cup was designed specifically for the line.

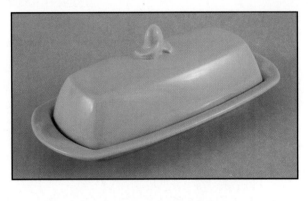

Chatham Gray covered butter $80.00–100.00.

Persian Cream salt and pepper shakers $10.00–16.00.

Chatham Gray Lu-Ray cream $20.00–30.00, and covered sugar $25.00–35.00.

Empire shape individual covered
sugar $35.00–45.00,
and cream $35.00–45.00.

Windsor Blue sauceboat
$12.00–15.00
using the pickle dish as an
underplate $20.00–28.00.

Windsor Blue muffin cover
$65.00–80.00
on an 8" plate $12.00–18.00.

Sauceboat and fixed stand
$12.00–15.00,
sauceboat $18.00–25.00,
in Lu-Ray Pastels.

*Lu-Ray double eggcup. The small
end is for soft boiled eggs, the
large end for poached
$12.00–18.00.*

*Lu-Ray Pastels cream soup cup and saucer
$68.00–85.00.*

*Flower vase in Persian Cream $90.00–125.00.
Sometimes called an epergne by collectors.*

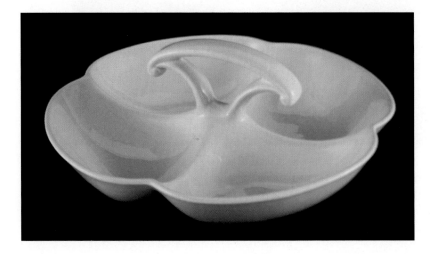

*Left: Bud urn $200.00–225.00.
Right: Bud vase $200.00–225.00.*

*Lu-Ray Pastels
Windsor Blue relish dish
$65.00–95.00.*

The original "chocolate set" design for the after-dinner coffee service, produced during 1939. From left: Sharon Pink individual cream $85.00–100.00, coffee pot $350.00–375.00, individual covered sugar $85.00–100.00, cups and saucers $70.00–95.00 ea. in all four colors trimmed in gold.

Original design for the individual covered sugar $85.00–100.00, and cream $85.00–100.00. Not all were trimmed in gold.

CHAPTER 3

COLLECTING LU-RAY PASTELS

Collecting Lu-Ray Pastels is more popular than ever before. One of the reasons collecting dinnerware is so enjoyable is that early 20th century American manufacturing practices provide clues to help identify, catalog, and date their products. In the course of their business, T.S.&T. left many clues for today's collectors.

Understanding Backstamps

Of course, Lu-Ray Pastels can be readily identified by its colors and shapes. But, in addition, many pieces are marked with a backstamp. Backstamps are trade and production marks. The Lu-Ray Pastels backstamp, identifying T.S.&T. as the manufacturer and with the distinctive Lu-Ray Pastels logo identifying the product, served to assure the customer they were buying the genuine article. It serves the same purpose for collectors today.

The Lu-Ray backstamp also had a quality control purpose, recording the month and year of manufacture and the kiln or line where the item was made. These dates have helped us piece together the history of the line.

Lu-Ray Pastels backstamp.

When production of Lu-Ray began almost every piece was marked. Even small items like the Empire-shape after-dinner cups, the bud vase and bud urn had full Lu-Ray backstamps including the month and year they were made. However, items lacking a flat surface, like the salt and pepper shakers and the inside surfaces of covers for pieces such as the sugar bowl, covered butter, and teapot were marked simply "U.S.A." By the early 1950s, fewer items were backstamped and by the end of Lu-Ray's production, only some of the 9" and 10" plates were marked.

T.S.&T may have felt that the possible loss of revenue from a competitor selling copies of Lu-Ray Pastels did not justify the cost of stamping each piece. Also, improvements in manufacturing by Taylor Smith & Taylor may have lessened the need for backstamps as an aid in quality control. Whatever the reasons, stamping the ware became viewed as a costly, nonessential step in the production process.

From left: Original design for the teapot $60.00–75.00, flower vase $90.00–125.00, original water jug with foot $50.00–70.00, compartment plate $18.00–25.00, and coaster $60.00–75.00.

The Lu-Ray Glaze

Another aspect of Lu-Ray that changed over time was the glaze. Collectors will notice the texture of the glaze and consistency of Lu-Ray Pastels' colors improved over the years of its production. The glaze of early Lu-Ray pieces is shinier than the subtly matted finish of later pieces.

Also, the color intensity of early Lu-Ray items tends to vary between batches. Edges and raised areas did not take the colors very well and show up white. This is easily noticed on bowls and plates. Later Lu-Ray production became much more uniform in color and texture, and these improvements coincided with the decreased use of backstamps in the early to mid-1950s.

Collecting Lu-Ray Pastels.
Left to right: relish dish $65.00–95.00,
cream soup cup and saucer $68.00–85.00,
teapot "flatspout" $60.00–75.00,
13" dish $13.00–18.00,
chop plate $20.00–30.00,
juice jug $100.00–130.00,
coaster $60.00–75.00,
flower vase $90.00–125.00.

In Search of the Rare Pastel

While many collectors like to assemble sets and examples of standard production dinnerware, others enjoy pursuing rarities, and Lu-Ray has its share. Some Lu-Ray Pastels items weren't big sellers and so had brief production runs making these pieces scarce. For example, the original design for the after-dinner coffee pot, cups, saucers, individual cream and sugar — the so called "chocolate set" — was only offered from about January 1939 to January 1940. At that time, it was replaced by the more familiar Empire-shape after-dinner coffee set.

T.S.&T. sales literature and internal memos suggest the teapot (curved spout) and chop plate were never made in Chatham Gray, but at least five gray teapots are known and a number of gray chop plates. While there wasn't enough demand to justify offering these as standard items, T.S.&T. made these to fill large special orders.

Other unusual items are 7" Laurel-shape serving platters and "fruit bowls" measuring six-and-one-half inches instead of the usual five inches and dipped in Lu-Ray Pastels glazes. These were definitely part of the Laurel line but are not known to have been standard items in Lu-Ray. More special orders? Most likely, since T.S.&T. would accept them if they could earn a profit.

A number of white after-dinner cups and saucers in the Lu-Ray shape have also been seen. These were intended to go with other lines as were the pink ones seen with the "Dwarf Pine" decal.

Perhaps the most puzzling rarity is the "handleless sugar bowl." Most, though not all, are in Lu-Ray colors and, unfortunately, none are marked. Each has the Empire-shape finial on its cover. Since the bottom and cover would have required the cost of special molds and production, it seems likely that this was a standard production item rather than a special order. We've heard that this piece could be a later restyling of the sugar bowl. We've also heard that they are marmalades. Whether these were actually intended for Lu-Ray or meant for another line is unknown. Perhaps a brochure or price list will surface which will solve the mystery.

Lu-Ray covered sugar $10.00–12.00 and "handleless sugar bowl."
It is difficult to determine values for the "handleless sugar bowls"
as they have not yet been established as Lu-Ray.

"Handleless sugar bowls."
The cover on the right, missing its bottom, has been decorated in bronze.

Lu-Ray after-dinner coffee cups and saucers on a handy "go along" carrier.
$8.00–12.00.

Lu-Ray Go-Alongs

There were many items made to go with Lu-Ray. Some were not T.S.&T. products but were made to complement the Lu-Ray Pastels line. Created by other companies, these items were marketed to appeal to Lu-Ray customers. Stemware sets, the Glassbake custard set, and carriers for after-dinner cups and saucers are good examples.

T.S.&T. did make their own "tidbit" trays by drilling plates and fitting them with metal stands. They may have made some in Lu-Ray. For a while, T.S.&T. owned a company called "Timbercraft" which made wood fittings and accessories to go with T.S.&T. lines.

Glassbake, USA glass custard cups may have been made to go with Lu-Ray Pastels.

CHAPTER 4

THE GRIFFIN

T.S.&T. from 1900 to 1930

Early Shapes

We call this chapter "The Griffin" because it was the symbol used as T.S.&T.'s first backstamp. The regal, winged lion, known as an English heraldic symbol, sat proudly on the back of much of T.S.&T. china until about 1910. It symbolizes the strong influence of the English on the American pottery market. English and other imported ware had dominated the American market since Colonial times. It wasn't until the griffin's final flight that American dinnerware was to come into its own.

Influenced by the English

According to T.S.&T. records, the first ware was produced in its Chester, West Virginia, plant in 1900. Since American dinnerware had not yet established itself as a quality product, T.S.&T., like other American potteries, copied English pottery forms and styles.

In fact, many of T.S.&T. potters and other American manufacturers' potters were English-born and trained. English pottery trade expressions, such as "baker" for an oval vegetable bowl and "nappy" for a round one were used by T.S.&T. and other U.S. potteries. T.S.&T. also used the "sterling weight" or "sterling pound" schedule to price its ware. This was an English system its potters were accustomed to using. For example, prices for Lu-Ray Pastels, Versatile, and Pebbleford were based on the "$8.00 per Pound Sterling List" in T.S.&T.'s January 1, 1942, Sterling Book.

Early Products

By 1908 other backstamps, such as "TST China," were beginning to be used. By 1915 T.S.&T. began to launch new shapes with trade or brand names like Latona and Verona (c.1915) followed by Avona China (c.1917), Pennova (c.1920), Belva China (c.1920), and Iona China (c.1920). The Paramount shape in both white and ivory bodies had been introduced by the late 1920s and proved, judging by the quantity of surviving pieces, to have been a popular dinnerware line. While few, if any, of these early lines identified themselves as "made in the USA," all of them were proudly signed by their maker, "T.S.&T."

Also, during this time, T.S.&T. produced items ranging from exquisite art pottery to utilitarian household articles such as bedpans. These items are rare.

Avona China backstamp.

THE COMPANY'S HISTORY

A plaque on display at the East Liverpool Museum of Ceramics has this to say about the history of The Taylor, Smith and Taylor Company:

"John N. Taylor and Charles A. Smith first organized the company in 1899, to produce semi-porcelain. Soon after the initial organization, Joseph Lee and two of Taylor's sons joined the firm which became known as Taylor, Lee and Smith. John Taylor intended to start his sons in the pottery business with this new venture. The company, blessed with ample capital, began construction of a modern new plant in Chester, West Virginia, a town directly across the river from East Liverpool. When Joseph Lee withdrew in 1901, the firm became known as Taylor, Smith and Taylor. After experiencing several years of unsatisfactory operations, in 1905, the pottery closed for over a year. In 1906 William Smith and his son purchased the Taylor interests and reorganized the idle company. They placed the plant in operation, retaining the firm's old name of Taylor, Smith and Taylor..."

Chester, West Virginia, the site of the new plant, was largely the creation of Chester A. Smith, for whom the town was named. Not only did Smith own the site of the factory but most of the residential and commercial lots, the trolley company, the amusement park, and other businesses. For many years the office staff of T.S.&T. kept the books for his real estate transactions.

By 1907, all of T.S.&T.'s operations had moved across the Ohio river from East Liverpool to Chester. A post office box was maintained in East Liverpool, however, to keep the company's official address in the capital of American dinnerware. The East Liverpool address was retained until later years when the bridge connecting Chester to East Liverpool was closed for repairs, making the trip to the post office inconvenient. The mailing address was then changed to Chester.

SHAPES vs. PATTERNS

When developing a new product, T.S.&T. usually thought in terms of the new shape or form the product would take instead of how it would be decorated. Once T.S.&T. came up with a new shape they would decorate it using whatever new or existing decals or hand-painted decoration they hoped would sell. Sometimes many different decorations would be tried to see which ones would be popular. Some combinations of shapes and decorations were so popular, like Lu-Ray, that they would sell for decades and are easy to find today. Others were immediate failures and are now rare.

Like T.S.&T., many enthusiasts assemble their collections of T.S.&T. by shapes. Exceptions are popular lines like Lu-Ray, Vistosa, and Pebbleford. We have organized our book the same way. In this and the following chapters you will find information about T.S.&T.'s wares listed by shape with examples of the most successful patterns.

COLLECTING EARLY T.S.&T.

T.S.&T.'s earliest wares, those marked with the griffin backstamp, are the most difficult group to find. Along with the other products of T.S.&T.'s early years, TST China and shapes Latona, Verona, Avona, Pennova, and Belva China, were made in smaller quantities and sold in fewer markets than T.S.&T.'s later products. The few surviving examples are often mistaken for the imported English ware which they copied. The passage of time and the relatively fragile bodies of these items also make them scarce, especially pieces in good condition.

Examples of Iona China, introduced about 1920, are more readily found than the other early shapes, suggesting it was made in larger quantities. Plates, especially platters, are the most easily found items in this shape. Paramount, in both white and ivory bodies, continued in production from the late 1920s into the early 1930s and sets of this shape may still be found or assembled in good condition. Since few collectors are currently seeking these wares, the prices are still low.

Griffin backstamp on an early T.S.&T. water jug.

T.S.&T.'s first backstamp, the griffin.

T.S.&T.'s salesman's postcard used for booking appointments with buyers. The caricature of the butler, considered tasteless and unprofessional today, was thought humorous in the early 1900s. Note the griffin logo superimposed under the firm's name.

Early 1900s fruit plate
with the griffin backstamp.

Early T.S.&T. water jug with the griffin backstamp.

Unknown Avona China pattern.
Covered casserole, sauceboat, pickle .
Dated 1–20.

Iona China backstamp.
Dated 4–22.

Floral border on Iona China shape. Dated 4–22. The severe crazing, or cracking, and staining of the glaze is, unfortunately, typical of the condition of many of the pieces from this period.

Iona China 7" plate.

Iona China platter.

Iona China backstamp.
Dated 4–24.

Iona China platter.

Iona China platter. Dated 4–24.

"Bluebird" pattern on Iona China.

Detail of "Bluebird" pattern and unknown pattern on Iona China.

*Heathertone pattern on
white Paramount shape, 1934.
10" plate $5.00, saucer $2.50, and
7" plate $4.00.*

*Paramount ivory body
backstamp reads:
"Pat. applied for"
under scroll, dated 11–29.*

*Heathertone pattern on a Paramount
shape baker $10.00.*

*Heathertone pattern on the Para-
mount shape $5.00.*

Paramount teapot $50.00.

Paramount plates with an ivory body. 6" plate $3.00, 7" plate $4.00, 10" plate $5.00.

Chester Hotel China backstamp.

Chester Hotel China platter. This line was designed for restaurants and institutions.

Taylor, Smith & Taylor Pottery, Chester, W. Va.

Postcard view dated 1912 of the T.S.&T. Chester, West Virginia, plant showing the early bottle type kilns.

CHAPTER 5

PREMIER POTTERS
OF AMERICA

1930 to 1955

Capitol, Laurel, Vogue, Delphian, Beverly, Fairway, Garland, Empire, and Plymouth

By the beginning of the 1930s, T.S.&T.'s products, like those of other U.S. potters, had gained acceptance by the American public. Unfortunately, the nation's economy had just entered the deepest economic depression in its history. The effects of the Great Depression disrupted the lives of all Americans, leaving most with a lot less money to spend. For many, necessities such as food and clothing were hard to obtain. Purchasing dinnerware was not a priority.

Stiff Competition for Dinnerware Sales

The Depression meant T.S.&T. had to work harder to successfully compete for consumers' dollars. As a result, T.S.&T. introduced more new shapes and patterns in the 1930s than during any other decade. Calling themselves the "Premier Potters of America," T.S.&T. also did more advertising in trade journals during this time than at any other period in its long history. All this was calculated to attract the attention of buyers from major department stores and catalog retailing houses.

The Popularity of Decals

Decals were used to dress up patterns and attract buyers. Many decals, if they proved popular, were used on more than one shape over many years. The "Rose Mist" decal, introduced in late 1930, appeared on the Paramount shape, a carry-over from the 1920s, and also on Capitol, a shape introduced in January 1930. "Dogwood," introduced in 1933, originally appeared on the Vogue shape, and on the Fairway shape, as late as 1942. "Pink Castle" first appeared in 1931, and was still being promoted in ads "for spring show tables" on the Garland shape in April 1941. Mixing existing decals with existing shapes was an inexpensive way of making "new" lines.

Some shapes were made in more than one body or color of the ware itself. While most wares were white, some were also made in ivory or rose.

A Variety of Backstamps

During the 1930s, T.S.&T. began using a standard backstamp for most of its lines rather than an individual one for each shape. Capitol, Lu-Ray, and Vistosa had their own backstamps, while Laurel, Vogue, Delphian, Beverly, Fairway, Garland, Empire, and Plymouth did not. From about 1930 to 1935, a simple backstamp, "TST Co.," in a notched rectangle was used on lines lacking their own backstamp. Beginning in about 1936, the legend "Taylor, Smith, Taylor" in a wreath was used and continued on these lines throughout their production. Almost all of these backstamps include the month and year that the ware was made which makes dating your collection very easy.

Introducing New Shapes

New lines were introduced to buyers at trade shows. The biggest shows were in January when buyers selected dinnerware to sell in the spring. August shows were also busy when buyers were making choices for their Christmas merchandise. T.S.&T. usually let buyers know that they had a new line to display. The month before each show they placed ads in the trade journals announcing the names of their new lines. Photographs were not included creating anticipation for the show.

Capitol

Capitol, the first new T.S.& T. shape of the 1930s, introduced in January 1930, seems difficult to find, suggesting a short production run. It has a distinctive backstamp with the U.S. capitol dome as its logo.

Laurel

Laurel, advertised as "an exclusive new shape potted to perfection," was one of T.S.&T.'s most successful shapes and was the basis of Empire and Lu-Ray. It was introduced at the Pittsburgh show in January 1933, and was instantly accepted by the public. Many new decals were designed for it into the early 1950s. It was, according to the company, "created by our art department, under the direction of J. Palin Thorley," a noted English ceramist and teacher who worked under contract for T.S.&T. during the 1930s. The very simple, light, modern shape was described as having "a narrower flange on dinner plates" giving a "larger serving surface," according to *China, Glass & Lamps* in 1933.

In addition, Laurel cups were noted for their added strength, having cast, or block, handles instead of the usual handles attached to the cup at only two points. These handles were easily broken off. All Laurel hollowware was footed to give it a formal look. In 1933, 32 piece sets sold retail for $4.95 and up.

Vogue

Vogue, advertised as a "lovely swirl shape," was another successful line created under the direction of J. Palin Thorley. Introduced in January 1934, at the Pittsburgh show, it continued in production into the early 1940s. Perhaps the most striking patterns were the "Dot" underglaze decorations, "Spiral Dot Green," "Polka Dot Blue," and "Border Dot Green," advertised in November 1934. Vogue's long production run makes it fairly easy to find.

Delphian

Delphian, made in both white and ivory bodies, appeared in 1935. "Delphian Rose," a pattern in blue or rose with a floral decal printed from a copper plate engraving, was in the style of English Staffordshire ware. The shape of the plates, with their embossed, checkered flanges, proved popular. But, unfortunately the hollowware was not a successful design. It resembled Victorian pottery and buyers were not interested in the line.

Beverly

In January 1936, Delphian plates, together with newly designed, square-footed, Art Deco-influenced hollowware was reintroduced as Beverly. Beverly continued to be available into the early 1940s. Interestingly, no credit for the design of either Delphian or Beverly was given in T.S.&T.'s ads. These shapes are not easily found.

Garland and Fairway

The Garland and Fairway shapes appeared in 1935. Garland, with its embossed border of leaves, was produced into the early 1950s and Fairway, with a scrolled edge and embossed border of trailing flowers, is known to have been produced until after World War II. Fairway is the more commonly found of the two shapes. Popular underglaze decorations such as "Petite Point," "Castle," "English Abbey," "Dogwood," and "Center Bouquet," have appeared on these shapes.

Empire

Empire, also by J. Palin Thorley, under contract for T.S.&T., was introduced in January 1936, in Pittsburgh. The Empire shape was actually new hollowware designed to go with the flat pieces from Thorley's Laurel shape. Empire hollowware is less formal than Laurel's, lacking a foot and more streamlined. Tea cups are the same for both lines. Empire hollowware is easily recognized by the bud-shaped finial on covered pieces such as the butter dish, sugar bowl, and casserole. The stylized bud shape is also incorporated into the design of the salt and pepper shakers. Not all hollowware was redesigned. The design of the nappy and baker remained the Laurel design. With few changes, the Empire shape is the Lu-Ray shape. Like Laurel, Empire, with many different patterns, continued to be manufactured into the mid 1950s.

Not only did Empire successfully compete against foreign manufacturers, it sometimes copied their lines. In October 1940, T.S.&T. advertised "Dutch Tulip" and "Blue Crocus." "Moderately priced underglaze patterns . . . are replacing imports in many china and gift departments," said T.S.&T. in their ad. But actually these patterns resemble Blue Ridge by American competitor, Southern Potteries. In December of 1940, Empire was offered with "ivory shoulders," ivory pieces with white centers closely resembling Japan's Noritake patterns of the late 1930s and 1940s.

Plymouth

Plymouth, the last new shape introduced during the 1930s, made its debut at the New York show at the Hotel Pennsylvania held July 11-17, 1937. Judging from the variety of examples available today, Plymouth seems to have been a hit. Made in white, ivory, and rose bodies, Plymouth appeared with many different decals on its rope-embossed shape until discontinued in the early 1940s.

Probably the most interesting pattern on Plymouth is "Mexican Fantasy." Advertised as "seven patterns — co-related Mexican subjects — made into one, lovely, smart attractive ensemble," "Mexican Fantasy" was clearly meant to compete with the Mexican lines by Homer Laughlin and other potters.

Foreign Competition

American potteries had temporary relief from foreign competition during and immediately after the second world war as foreign potteries had to be rebuilt. T.S.&T. continued offering the Lu-Ray Pastels line, Garland, Fairway, Laurel, and Empire with new and some pre-war decorations until, by the late 1940s, foreign competition gradually returned. Many of the new lines from overseas offered new, post-modern, "Jet Age" designs, forcing T.S.&T. to respond with new shapes of their own.

In a March 1941, advertisement for Lu-Ray Pastels T.S.&T. advised "astute department stores and shops" to stock up "heavily" on their wares to prepare for "the approaching period of greatly increased national income."

While prosperity would ultimately return, changes in American tastes and a more informal lifestyle would eliminate all but the Laurel and Empire shapes and the Lu-Ray line from production by the early 1950s. By the mid-1950s the Laurel and Empire shapes were dropped making Lu-Ray Pastels the only survivor of the many products T.S.&T. designed to compete for the few consumer dollars available during the Great Depression.

COLLECTING PATTERNS OF THE 1930S AND 1940S.

Of T.S.&T.'s "Premier Potters of America" era, the 1930s and 1940s, there are many patterns available on each of the shapes including, Capitol, Laurel, Vogue, Delphian, Beverly, Fairway, Garland, Empire, and Plymouth. We are sure we have not seen them all! The Capitol shape is the rarest from this period. We were unable to locate examples for this book, although they may be more plentiful in other parts of the country where their sales may have been stronger. Delphian, offered for only one year before being absorbed into Beverly, is not easily found.

Empire and Laurel are the most common of the Depression and wartime era shapes, followed by Fairway, Plymouth, Garland, and Vogue. These shapes are often still available in sets or fragments of sets and, with patience, collectors can reassemble as many place settings as they desire. Prices for these decaled lines are currently reasonable since collectors are just beginning to discover these patterns.

Children's sets were also offered during this period. A Popeye the Sailor cup and bowl were advertised by T.S.&T. in 1937. Later Raggedy Ann and Howdy Doody appeared on children's sets. These items are very rare. Even damaged pieces are valued by collectors.

*Late 1920s – early 1930s
T.S.&T. backstamp.*

*Post 1935 T.S.&T. backstamp with "Premier"
series stamp. The premier stamp was used on a
number of lines.*

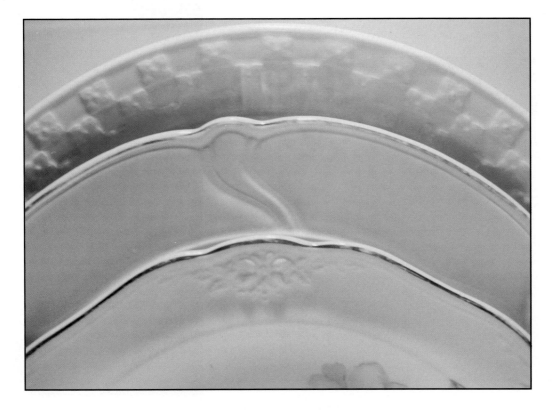

*Detail of 1930s T.S.&T. shapes.
From inside: Unknown, Vogue, and Delphian or Beverly.*

Detail of Plymouth shape (inside) against the Garland shape.

Early pattern on Laurel 10" plate 1934, $2.50.

Floral decoration on a Laurel or Empire pickle $7.00.

*"Center Bouquet" pattern on
Laurel or Empire saucer $1.50,
and coupe soup $2.00.*

Decal and gilt decorated 7" plate, Laurel or Empire $2.00.

*Floral decal on Laurel or Empire 9" plate
with gilt decoration $2.00.*

*Laurel or Empire
shape bowls.
From left:
fruit $1.50,
coupe soup $2.00,
and fruit $1.50.
All dated 1940–1948.*

Late 1930s pattern on Laurel or Empire saucer $1.75.

Perfect for a Thanksgiving dinner, an unidentified pattern 6" plate on Laurel or Empire $1.75.

Backstamp on 6" Thanksgiving motif. Decal plate dated 11–49. Nationwide Consumers distributed and may have contracted for this ware. $1.75.

This nappy must have been a favorite serving bowl on Thanksgiving. On the Laurel or Empire shape, this is dated 7–52 $4.00.

"Appalachian Heirloom" on Bonnie
(tu-tone Laurel or Empire). Dated 11–54.

"Dogwood" pattern on Laurel or
Empire 13" platter $6.00.

"Appalachian Heirloom" pattern on
"Tu-tone" Bonnie (Laurel or
Empire). Early 1950s.
$2.00 and $1.75, respectively.

"Appalachian Heirloom" pattern on
"Tu-tone" Bonnie (really Laurel or
Empire) cup and saucer $3.50.

Covered casserole in "Rose Lattice"
on the Laurel shape $25.00.

"Rose Lattice" teacup and saucer on the
Laurel shape $3.50.

"Silhouette decal" on the Laurel shape.
Left: teacup and tea saucer $12.00, right: St. Denis cup and saucer $42.00.
These were special ordered by the Cook Coffee Company and the
Standard Coffee Company for use as premiums.

Laurel cream $15.00, and covered sugar $20.00 in "Silhouette" or "Taverne."
These were given away as premiums by the Cook Coffee Company and
The Standard Coffee Company.

"Silhouette" 13" dish $30.00,
7" dish $15.00, and baker $30.00
on the Laurel shape.

Coupe soup $15.00, butter dish bottom $50.00, large fruit or cereal bowl $20.00,
fruit bowl $7.00, all "Silhouette" on Laurel.

"Silhouette," also known as "Taverne" plates on the Laurel shape.
10" $25.00, 9" $10.00, 8" $20.00, 7" $15.00.

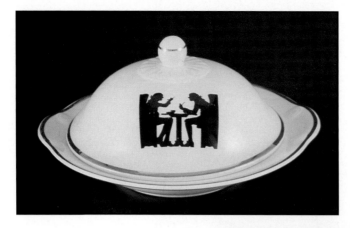

"Silhouette" covered butter dish on the Laurel shape $150.00.

"Silhouette" decal on a Vogue nappy. This is backstamped 6–35. $25.00.

Vogue 7" plate $2.50, coupe soup $2.50, 10" plate $3.00, fruit $2.00.

Sauceboat $7.50, and covered sugar $5.50, Vogue shape.

Covered casserole in the Vogue shape $27.00.

Tea saucer and teacup in Vogue $4.50.

"Heathertone" 10" plate on the Vogue shape $3.00.

Delphian or Beverly 10" plate $3.00.

Rose bodied Garland shape 9" plate
with unknown decal and platinum decoration $2.00.

"English Abbey" pattern on a Fairway shape 10" plate $12.50.
"English Abbey" backstamps do not mention T.S.&T.

"Center Bouquet" in Rose decal
on the Fairway shape 10" plate $12.50.

Unknown decal on a Fairway shape cream.
This same pattern also appeared on the
Empire shape during the 1940s $3.50.

"Dogwood" pattern on a Fairway shape platter $8.00.

Floral decal on an unidentified shape similar to Fairway. The nappy $3.50, coupe soup $2.50, 10" plate $3.00, and 6" plate $2.25, are all dated 1932 to 1936.

"Petite Point" and an unknown pattern on the Fairway shape, platter $8.00, 6" plate $2.25.

"Delphian Rose" decal in blue on 9" Fairway plate $10.00.

"Center Bouquet" pattern on the Fairway shape cup $5.00, and Laurel or Empire saucer $3.50.

Unidentified but popular pattern on Empire. Production dates are from 1936–1946, suggesting a long production run. This decal has also been seen on Vogue. 6" plate $1.75, teapot $25.00.

Gilt number reflects gilt decoration on this Empire cream $4.00.

Empire cream with floral decal dated 4–49 $4.00.

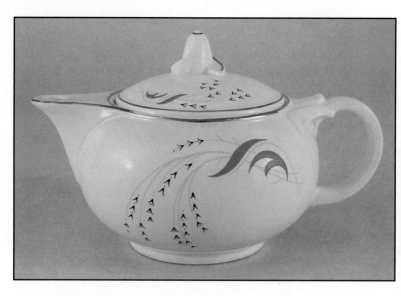

Empire covered sugar with platinum decoration.
Dated 12–41 $5.00.

"Red Wheat" teapot in the Empire shape, 1938 $25.00.

Decaled, gilt decorated
line in Empire.

Over-decorated Empire covered butter $10.00.

*Plymouth cake plate with floral decal
and gilt decoration $10.00.*

Plymouth covered sugar $5.50.

*"Mexican Fantasy" on Plymouth.
Cake plate $20.00, 10" plate $12.50, 6" plate $6.00.*

"Chinese Temple"
fruit $2.00, 7" plate $2.50,
on the Plymouth shape.
Dated 8–37.

Plymouth cake plate with
unknown stylized floral decal
$10.00.

Pastoral backstamp.

Pastoral bread and butter
plate $2.50, fruit $2.50.
These were given away as
premiums by Quaker Oats
and were ordered from
T.S.&T. and other potteries,
circa 1955.

Some T.S.&T. pieces were decorated by firms specializing in gilt decoration. This one was decorated by LaMode China, backstamped by T.S.&T. 1939.

Both the pattern and shape are unknown on this 1934 covered sugar.

Another example of gilt-decorated ware decorated by someone other than T.S.&T. Eastern China added their backstamp in gold to this 3–41 Laurel or Empire plate.

While the decal on these custard cups matches those on an Empire shape set, these are believed to be Universal Pottery products.

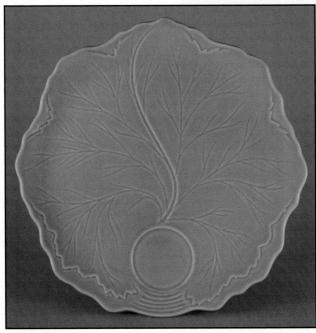

Leaf Fantasy luncheon plate in Lu-Ray Surf Green. These were sold in sets of mixed Lu-Ray colors. The round compartment at the base holds a matching teacup $15.00.

THE PLACE } New York Show Hotel Pennsylvania Room 650-652

THE TIME } July 10th to 19th

THE LINE } The Taylor, Smith & Taylor Co.

FEATURING DELPHIAN IVORY IN MANY NEW PATTERNS.

A. H. Dornan   *W. J. Kelly*   *Bryce Palmer*

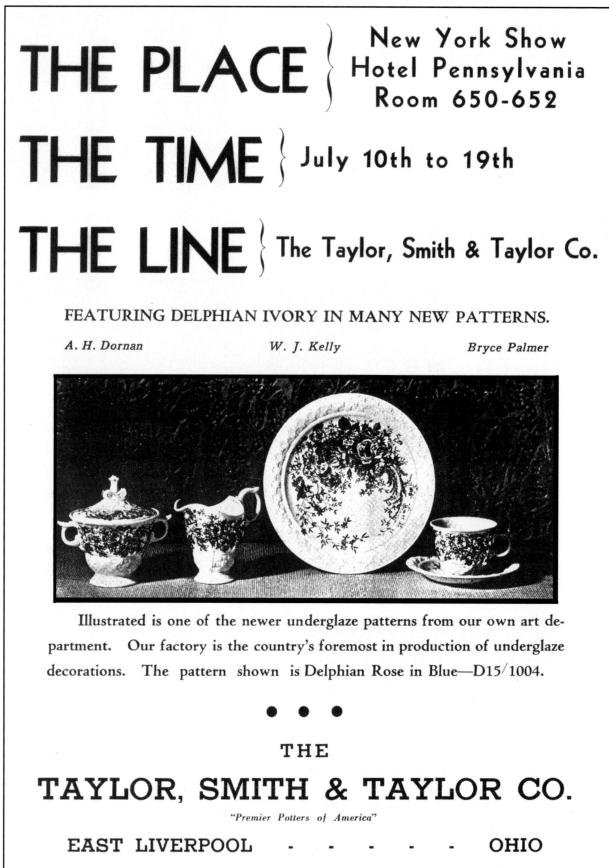

Illustrated is one of the newer underglaze patterns from our own art department.   Our factory is the country's foremost in production of underglaze decorations.   The pattern shown is Delphian Rose in Blue—D15/1004.

● ● ●

THE
TAYLOR, SMITH & TAYLOR CO.
"Premier Potters of America"

EAST LIVERPOOL - - - - - OHIO

New Fall Lines Also on Display at Hotel Morrison, Chicago, July 29th to August 10th.

June 1935 ad for Delphian in an ivory body featuring the "Delphian Rose" pattern in blue.

THESE TWO NEW SHAPES

With Many New Treatments Will Meet Your Dinnerware Requirements

Distinctive and attractive is this Blue Gingham Plaid treatment on the stately EMPIRE shape. One of many patterns to make your customers buy. It's No. EOI 2/1223.

Yellow and gold to brighten any table is the combination in this charming pattern on the BEVERLY. Daisies in yellow combine tastefully with a lace border in gold. Truly, a winner. It's No. BOI 5/1222.

Our Salesmen are Glad To Serve You

A. H. Dornan—The East.
W. J. Kelly—New England
D. E. Sanford Co., Los Angeles and San Francisco.
D. D. Otstott, Inc.—Dallas.
Ben Sinsheimer — Portland, Oregon.
Miller & Gray—Minneapolis
A. L. Hungerford—St. Petersburg, Fla.
L. H. Davis—Findlay, O.
A. W. Anderson — Ironwood, Mich.
L. A. Fallen—Seward, Neb.
L. Y. Ramsey, Jamestown, N. Y.

THE TAYLOR, SMITH & TAYLOR COMPANY

"PREMIER POTTERS OF AMERICA"

EAST LIVERPOOL, OHIO

Bryce Palmer, Sales Manager

March 1936 ad run in China, Glass and Lamps *for the Empire and Beverly shapes.*

October 1940 ad for "Dutch Tulip" and "Blue Crocus" on Laurel or Empire. These patterns, while touted as "replacing imports" actually resemble Southern Potteries' Blue Ridge designs.

NEW CLASSIC DECORATIONS ON IVORY SHOULDERS

Harmonizing with today's classic interiors are the two patterns illustrated. "Scroll Border" has scrolls and garlands with flowerette center. "Daphne" is a gold stamp in laurel motif. Both decorations are on ivory shoulders.

UNDERGLAZE

In the strong line of underglaze patterns is the beautiful "Dogwood." A favorite for seven years, it is destined for many years more.

LU-RAY PASTELS

New items have been added to the "Lu-Ray" pastels, those gorgeous soft tones on dinnerware and special items.

AT PITTSBURGH EXHIBIT

SUITE 635

HOTEL WILLIAM PENN

THE TAYLOR, SMITH & TAYLOR CO.

PREMIER POTTERS OF AMERICA

EAST LIVERPOOL, OHIO

This December 1940 trade journal ad shows two toned decoration on Laurel imitating Japan's Noritake china. Also illustrated is the "Dogwood" pattern on the Fairway shape. Dogwood was a J. Palin Thorley design under contract with T.S.&T.

71

• From the Taylor, Smith & Taylor Company is this handsome, formal dinnerware design on the "Laurel" shape. It has six graduated lines in coin gold on the rim, with gold foot and handles on the hollow pieces.

Laurel 10" plate, cream soup cup and saucer decorated with six graduated lines in coin gold, gold foot and handles. Shown in China, Glass and Lamps, *September 1941.*

CHAPTER 6

VISTOSA

1938 to circa 1942

Trade show display used by T.S.&T. to introduce Vistosa, January 1938.
Original art by Erich Lorenz v. Benndorff from period photographs.

Summarizing the year, the August 1938 issue of *China, Glass and Lamps* declared "the kitchenware theme – color and more color." T.S.&T.'s introduction of Vistosa contributed to this colorful theme.

Red, Green, Yellow, and Blue

At the January New York China, Glass and Housewares Show "a brand new line of solid-color ware made its bow to the market" reported *China, Glass and Lamps*. The reporter went on to describe T.S.&T.'s Vistosa, as a line in "the four popular colors – red, green, yellow, and blue. . ." with a shape having "a scallop embossment on the rim." The magazine described the latest developments in other U.S. potteries' lines, mentioning Homer Laughlin's Harlequin, Paden City's Caliente in "tangerine, turquoise, green, sapphire, and lemon," and Pacific Clay Products' new "Coralitos ware. . . mission ivory, cielito blue, dorado yellow, and verdigo green." T.S.&T. was entering a crowded market.

The January 1938 brochure's price list gives the pieces in the line as follows:

Teacups	Chop Plates, 15"
Tea Saucers	Covered Sugars
Plates, 10"	Creams
Plates, 9"	Teapots, 6-cup
Plates, 7"	Footed Salad Bowl, 12"
Plates, 6"	Water Jug, 2-quart
Coupe Soups	Salt Shaker
Lug Handled Soups	Pepper Shaker
Fruits, 5"	Footed Egg Cup
Nappy, 8½"	After-Dinner Coffee Cup
Chop Plates, 12"	After-Dinner Coffee Saucer

A sauceboat was added to the line sometime after Vistosa's introduction.

Items made in red were priced roughly 20% higher than those in green, blue, or yellow reflecting the higher cost of the red's raw materials. Today, collectors will find that the prices are uniform for all four colors.

By March 1938 *China Glass and Lamps* was able to report "Shipments of 'Vistosa' ware to department stores have been increasing, including re-orders as the result of consumer acceptance." Despite these favorable reviews and the assertion in a May 1938 ad that "Vistosa is selling profitably wherever it is displayed," the line appears to have quickly become overshadowed by Homer Laughlin's Fiesta and the immediate success of Lu-Ray Pastels. No further mention of Vistosa has been found in advertising after June 1939, when it was mentioned in a T.S.&T. ad along with "1939's leader," Lu-Ray Pastels.

It is not known exactly when Vistosa was discontinued. It is believed to have been dropped in the early to mid-1940s when many lines that were no longer profitable were discontinued.

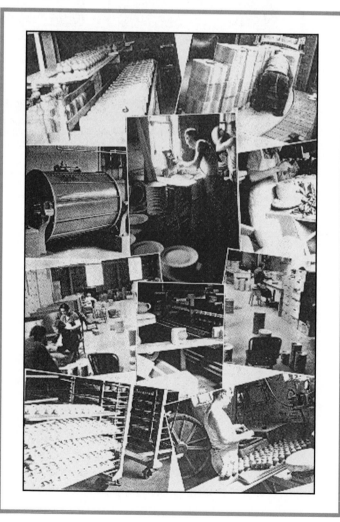

Vistosa in production at T.S.&T. These photos, without individual captions, accompanied the article "Viewing Vistosa" in China, Glass and Lamps, *February 1938.*

VIEWING VISTOSA

Reprinted with permission from the February 1938 issue of *China, Glass and Lamps*

In offering their new 'Vistosa' ware in bright colors, the Taylor, Smith & Taylor Co., manufacturing potters at East Liverpool, believe they have developed an exceptional product for the hostess who delights in gay surroundings, whether it be morning, noon, evening, or night.

'Vistosa' ware is an entirely new product. In order to make it the Taylor, Smith & Taylor Co. had to add to their productive facilities. This was done so that the bright colors of Vistosa — red, blue, yellow, and green — could be protected and their uniformity assured. With such care behind the product, the Taylor Smith & Taylor Co. believes the consumers will find in the ware something to cherish and something of joy and good taste.

From the Spanish, known for years for their affection for gay colors, comes the word 'Vistosa.' A literal translation of it is 'to brighten; to make cheerful.' And that is the aim of the Vistosa service as developed by the Taylor, Smith & Taylor Co.

The pieces comprising the Vistosa array are such that from it, colorful combinations may be made up for breakfast, for luncheon, for parties, for buffet occasions. There are four sizes in plates, two types of soups, teacup and saucer, egg cup, and sugar, and cream pitcher as well as the service items such as two sizes of chop plates, a salad bowl, a teapot, and a water pitcher as well as salt and pepper shakers.

Vistosa ware is the product of long months of development and experimentation. It is made of domestic clays and has an unusually tough body. The colors are uniform, true and enduring and the ware is craze-proof — at least, tests in the ceramic laboratories at the pottery have not disclosed otherwise.

Featuring Vistosa ware is an appealing embossed border. The embossment is in a double panel effect, adding a distinctive touch to the simple lines of the shape.

The body, the colors, and the system of production were developed by executives and the ceramic engineering department of the Taylor, Smith & Taylor Co. Because the handling of colors necessitates extreme care all along the line from the forming of the clay pieces to its packing, a new unit was added to the pottery layout. This adjoins the main decorating shop and is handy to the packing department.

Vistosa ware, as it is manufactured, is kept away from the other products of the Taylor, Smith & Taylor pottery. The colors are prepared in part of the new unit. The equipment for mixing each shade has its main drum painted in the color of the material it mixes. Each batch of color material is carefully selected and the mixing is supervised closely.

The extreme care in the manufacturing process is felt to be required so that matching of colors may be made without difficulty and that Vistosa colors will be uniform from the first shipment to the last. The most improved system of applying color has been installed in the new unit. The Vistosa ware moves progressively forward from the mixing of the clay to the wrapping for shipment.

In the final firing of the ware, which sets the colors irrevocably, a special circular, continuous kiln has been placed on the new unit. The smaller kiln offers greater facility for careful checking and control of the heat necessary to bring out the colors and to burn them thoroughly into the complete ware. All the Vistosa ware is placed in saggers for its final trip through the kiln. Saggers are containers of rough clay and their purpose is to afford more uniform firing and to protect the ware fully.

After the saggers are emptied of their colorful burden after passing through the kiln, each piece is inspected carefully. Any rough edges or even minute collections of clay or color are removed so that there is no danger of the ware scratching finely polished surfaces.

All of the illustrations accompanying this view of Vistosa ware were made in the Taylor, Smith & Taylor plant. They give a glimpse of the care required as well as of the equipment needed to produce an attractive and beautiful ware.

The four color shades which mark Vistosa — red, blue, green, and yellow — were selected so that they might contrast tastefully without clashing. With the four colors, it is possible to make innumerable gay combinations for a small bridge luncheon as well as for a major social occasion.

ORIGINAL VISTOSA SALES BROCHURE
January 1938

Vistosa is the modern hostess' stepping stone to smartness! It offers her virtually unending possibilities for table decoration...solid colors to combine with the popular colored table linen...contrasting colors to blend beautifully with surrounding decorative effects...Vistosa will make each meal a thrill...each setting a masterpiece of clever table decoration. And you have four lovely colors from which to choose!

You may prefer the dignified blue, the soft green, the vivacious red, or the warm yellow. Whichever you select will definitely add a final note of charm and friendliness to your table. Each may be used in combination with the other, offering an increased range of color blendings. Each item is priced separately enabling one to build a complete set in the pieces and colors desired.

Vistosa is bright...Vistosa is cheerful...Vistosa is gay... the very name describes the refreshing atmosphere it creates in the home. The vivid colors and the singing beauty of Vistosa will give to your table an alluring freshness...a captivating atmosphere...the perfect answer to the quest of every smart hostess! Vistosa has the qualities of a thoroughbred! Made from the finest clays in America, designed and shaped into pieces of loveliness by skilled craftsmen...craze proof...true, enduring colors...it brings you the sturdiness and simple beauty that strikes the keynote of modern pottery. Vistosa with its appealing embossed border motif is a combination of refinement, beauty, and unparalleled smartness. For breakfast, luncheon, dinner, or informal use, Vistosa gives an ensemble of harmonizing colors adding charm to any table.

COLLECTING VISTOSA

Vistosa is the most eagerly sought T.S.&T. product after Lu-Ray Pastels. Advertised as durable, its glazes and colors have held up well over the last 55 years. Damaged pieces tend to be chipped rather than cracked, crazed, or faded. The demand among collectors, coupled with its relatively small production, makes Vistosa hard to find outside of dealers specializing in the line. Vistosa is not an inexpensive line to collect and the prices for some items are higher than those for Lu-Ray. Lug and coupe soup bowls and 10" plates are the most difficult items to find. Sauceboats, apparently added after Vistosa's introduction, are very rare. While somewhat costly, a reassembled set of Vistosa makes a strikingly beautiful display.

Vistosa serving pieces:
Blue water jug $75.00–85.00,
12" green chop plate $30.00–40.00,
15" red chop plate $40.00–50.00,
yellow nappy $40.00–50.00.
While T.S.&T. catalogued the large
chop plate as 15", it actually mea-
sures 14".

Vistosa backstamp.

Incised mark on a Vistosa cream.

Vistosa 9" plate $15.00–20.00,
7" plate $12.00–18.00, 6" plate $10.00–15.00,
after-dinner coffee cup and saucer $45.00–55.00.

*Vistosa salt and pepper shakers
$20.00–30.00.*

*Rare Vistosa sauceboat $100.00–125.00.
These were added after the introduction
of Vistosa and are not shown in the
January 1938 brochure.*

*Vistosa teapots in
yellow and green
$80.00–100.00.*

Tea time in Vistosa. Teacups and saucers $15.00–22.00 ea. in all four colors with a yellow teapot $80.00–100.00.

Left: after-dinner coffee cup and saucer $45.00–55.00, Right: Vistosa teacup and saucer $15.00–22.00.

Teacups and saucers and after-dinner cups and saucers in Vistosa.

Covered sugar $20.00–25.00 and cream $15.00–20.00, in red Vistosa.

*Red Vistosa, Clockwise:
covered sugar $20.00–25.00,
cream $15.00–20.00,
teacup with saucer $15.00–22.00,
coupe soup $20.00–25.00,
9" plate $15.00–20.00,
6" plate $10.00–15.00,
salt and pepper shakers $20.00–30.00.*

*Breakfast setting in green Vistosa.
Clockwise:
salt and pepper shakers $20.00–30.00,
cup and saucer $15.00–22.00,
egg cup $25.00–30.00,
7" plate $12.00–18.00,
9" plate $15.00–20.00,
fruit $10.00–15.00,
6" plate $10.00–15.00.*

Vistosa bowls. From left:
coupe soup $20.00–25.00, fruit $10.00–15.00,
nappy $40.00–50.00, lug soup $25.00–30.00.

Vistosa 7" plate $12.00–18.00, 9" plate $15.00–20.00, 6" plate $10.00–15.00.

15" chop plate $40.00–50.00, 12" chop plate $30.00–40.00 in Vistosa.

Blue Vistosa nappy $40.00–50.00.

Vistosa footed salad bowl $175.00–200.00.

Vistosa egg cups $25.00–30.00.

CHAPTER 7

CORAL-CRAFT

1939

Coral-Craft made its appearance at the Chicago Home Furnishings Show and at the Pittsburgh China and Glass Show in January 1939. As described in *China, Glass and Lamps*, it was distinguished by "an eye-compelling new decoration, enamel-like in effect, done by a process created by the factory—showing inlaid designs in white against a pale coral body." Collectors will recognize the body as Sharon Pink Lu-Ray.

Coral-Craft Patterns

"Five different patterns were introduced in this form of decoration," continued the magazine. "A laurel band at the edge; a floral border; a maple leaf; tulips; or a Chinese temple in the center." It is not known if the line included items which had just been added to the Lu-Ray Pastels line, i.e. the flower vase, relish dish, after-dinner or "chocolate" coffee set, and egg cups. T.S.&T. placed ads for Coral-Craft in the trade journals only during 1939, and it is possible that the line was discontinued as early as 1940.

Coral-Craft teapot in the Tulip pattern $45.00–60.00.

Coral-Craft backstamp.

COLLECTING CORAL-CRAFT

Coral-Craft, on the Lu-Ray body, is an attractive line but its short production life makes it a challenge for any collector. Serving pieces seem more common than plates, cups, or saucers in this line.

CHAPTER 8

CONVERSATION

Designed by Walter Dorwin Teague
1950 to 1954

By the end of the 1940s, with the war over, potters in Europe and Asia began to rebuild their factories and export their wares to the lucrative American market. Although just a trickle at first, imports soon became a flood that would put many American potteries out of business.

The Response to Imported Pottery

Foreign potteries had the advantage of cheap labor which allowed them to sell their pottery for less than American manufacturers. To compete, T.S.&T. had its engineers design some of the most advanced pottery manufacturing machines in the world, replacing hand labor with less costly machine labor wherever possible. This trend would continue for the rest of T.S.&T.'s history.

Industrial Design Comes to the Pottery Industry

The imported wares had innovative new designs. T.S.&T. responded by contracting "the Dean of Industrial Designers," Walter Dorwin Teague (1883–1960) to create a new dinnerware shape.

Industrial designers are responsible for giving many of the everyday objects in our lives the appearances they have today. As technology created many new machines for the home and office, manufacturers soon learned that giving them attractive forms to complement their useful functions made them more salable. During the Depression years, Teague, along with contemporaries like Norman Bel Geddes, Raymond Loewy, and Henry Dreyfuss, combined Modernism with everything from locomotives to household appliances. The round, speedy-looking, striped appearance they created was called "streamlining." This was the basis of the aerodynamic look we associate with 1930s and 1940s design.

Conversation Makes its Debut

The dinnerware shape Teague designed to debut in 1950 was Conversation. Its pieces are squared and its hollowware low profile in contrast with the streamlined wares it replaced. The name of the shape may have been inspired by a feature magazine article called "Conversation" written by Mrs. Teague.

Many of the patterns offered on the Conversation shape included "Green Tutone," having the flange of the plates and exterior of the hollowware in dark green. At least sixteen patterns were offered, including "Day Lily," "Cockerel," "Magnolia," "Oakleaf," "Coffee Tree," and "King O'Dell," a jack-in-the pulpit decal in "Green Tutone" which is the easiest pattern to find today. Conversation has also been found dipped in Lu-Ray Pastels' Sharon Pink and Windsor Blue.

Production of Conversation continued through 1954, and is believed to have ended with the introduction of the more formal version of Versatile in 1955. Despite its few years in production, Conversation, in its many patterns, is readily available for collectors today.

WALTER DORWIN TEAGUE

Teague began his career as an artist designing advertising illustrations for magazines. His first industrial design commission was in 1928, for Kodak cameras. He and his associates went on to design automobiles, gas stations, railroad cars, airliner interiors, gas furnaces, furniture, department store showrooms, and magazines. He designed every type of glass from pickle jars to Steuben crystal.

Eventually, his repertoire extended from industrial engines to delicate silk fabrics. As Teague himself stated in a 1936 issue of *Arts and Decoration*, "painting and sculpture are art but so is the making of kitchen sinks and pickle bottles."

Based in Manhattan, the senior partner of Walter Dorwin Teague Associates became famous for his designs for the then-popular World's Fairs. Teague designed the Ford Building for the San Diego World's Fair in 1935, the Ford and Texaco Buildings for the Dallas World's Fair in 1936, and the Ford Building for the Miami World's Fair in 1937. He also designed exhibits for Ford, duPont, and US Steel in San Francisco in 1939. For the famous 1939 World's Fair held in New York, Teague served as a member of the design board, as well as designed buildings and exhibits for Kodak, Consolidated Edison, NCR, Ford, US Steel, and duPont.

In his day, Teague was also known as an author. He wrote a book about his work, *Design This Day* (1940) and, with his second wife, Ruth, a murder mystery, *You Can't Ignore Murder* in 1942.

COLLECTING CONVERSATION

Conversation is fast becoming a popular line with collectors. Its unusual form and its association with famous industrial designer Walter Dorwin Teague contribute to its increasing scarcity. For now, complete and partial sets may still be found, especially in the "King O'Dell" or, as it is often called by collectors, "jack-in-the-pulpit" pattern. Solid colored Conversation, dipped in Lu-Ray Pastels' colors, is a most desirable type and the most difficult to locate.

Conversation backstamp dated 9–50.

"Coffee Tree" dinner plate on Conversation $2.50.

"King O' Dell" covered casserole in Conversation $25.00.

"King O' Dell" pattern cream and covered sugar on Conversation $8.00.

*"King O' Dell" pattern
on Conversation.*

*Coffee server in "King O' Dell"
pattern on Conversation $20.00.*

*Platter in the "King O' Dell"
pattern on Conversation
$5.00.*

"King O' Dell" fruit $1.50, oval vegetable $6.00, round vegetable $3.00, on the Conversation shape.

Conversation baker dipped in Lu-Ray's Windsor Blue $6.00.

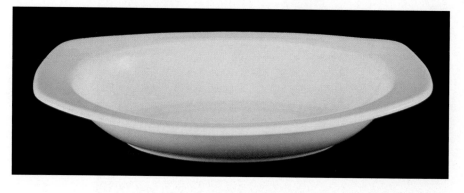

Side view of Conversation baker.

*Wildly decorated souvenir
dinner plate on Conversation
$2.50.*

*Covered sugar in unknown pattern
on Conversation $5.00.*

*Souvenir pattern on a Conversation dinner plate
$2.50.*

*Attractive, unknown pattern on
Conversation dinner plate $2.50.*

Unidentified patten in "tu-tone" Conversation.
Cream $3.00, covered sugar $5.00, coffee server $20.00.

Conversation, clockwise:
dinner plate $2.50, bread and butter plate $1.75,
cup and saucer $3.50, fruit $1.50.
Pattern unknown.

Conversation dinner plate in unknown pattern $2.50.

CHAPTER 9

AMERICA'S MOST VERSATILE DINNERWARE

Versatile
1952 to circa 1965

While Walter Dorwin Teague's Conversation shape was successful, T.S.&T.'s management felt more new designs were needed for the company to remain competitive. For the first time, T.S.&T. decided to employ a full time designer. John Gilkes was hired for this new position around 1950. He joined the small art department located in a former home across the street from the plant.

Introducing the Versatile Shape

Gilkes quickly made a name for himself by designing Versatile, a coupe shape with a spare, low-profile design. T.S.&T. introduced Versatile to the public in 1952. More than just an appealing modern design, Versatile's form followed what Gilkes believed would be its function: for casual or formal dining in the kitchen, den, patio, or dining room. Its plates were intended to look equally at home with a salad or a sandwich, its bowls with soup or a dip, serving pieces with mashed potatoes or potato chips.

Informal Lifestyles

Gilkes realized that American lifestyles, including eating habits, were becoming more informal. Formal meals, served in the dining room, were becoming less common. Dining rooms in new homes were becoming smaller as kitchens grew larger, reflecting that most meals and family life were centered in the kitchen. With the advent of frozen and convenience foods, meal times became less rigid and snacking more common, especially in front of the TV. Barbecues and eating outside also became more popular as patios were added to homes all over the country. Taking all of this into account, Versatile's simple, aerodynamic form and its multiple-use serving pieces were made to appeal to this new market.

Multiple Uses

Christened "Versatile" for its multiple uses, Gilkes used the distinctive profile of its covered casserole as the logo for the new shape, incorporating it as part of its backstamp. When first produced, all pieces were backstamped, except for tea cups and salt and pepper shakers. The backstamps included the month and year of manufacture. Gradually fewer pieces were backstamped until, by the close of production in the mid–1960s, only dinner plates were marked.

The best known line in the Versatile shape is Gilkes' Pebbleford. New items on the Versatile shape were brought out as part of the Pebbleford line and sometimes these were also offered with other Versatile lines.

In addition to being a "versatile" line for the homemaker, Versatile proved to be equally adaptable to a wide range of customers. While conceived as a casual line, Gilkes recognized that there still remained a market for a more formal service.

A More Formal Version of the Versatile Shape

In 1955 T.S.&T. discontinued Conversation and retired the then antique Empire shape. Gilkes replaced it with a more formal, traditionally-styled version of Versatile. Most items, including plates, platters, saucers, and vegetable bowls remained the same. Teacups, covered casseroles, creams and sugars, salt and pepper shakers, and coffee servers were given a less severe, more traditional design.

Some of these formal Versatile lines, like Dwarf Pine, included such old fashioned items as after-dinner coffee cups and saucers on the Lu-Ray shape. Many of these lines have the "tu-tone" look of Conversation, featuring a decal on white coupe shape pieces with hollowware of white and a contrasting yellow, turquoise, or gray.

Meanwhile, the original, casual post-modern version of Versatile continued to be produced. By the late 1950s solid-colored lines in the tradition of Lu-Ray Pastels were available. A line on the Versatile shape has been seen in Lu-Ray's Persian Cream and Surf Green as well as in a rich pastel blue. The name of the line is unknown.

Versatile continued to evolve throughout its production. Teacups in its casual version became rounded and then taller. Serving pieces became less severe, becoming more abstract and free-form. Ultimately, it evolved into other shapes. The formal design hollowware was continued in the Classic shape.

The flat, coupe shape pieces became the basis for Gilkes's Ever Yours shape. The forms of some late Versatile serving pieces are similar to Ever Yours. This makes it difficult to distinguish between them. Matching these pieces by their decal to those having an identifying backstamp is the best method for positive identification.

By the mid-1960s both versions of Versatile were discontinued. Gilkes had been very successful in creating a product that appealed to most segments of the dinnerware market with a minimum of costly retooling and labor.

COLLECTING VERSATILE

Among the lines in the Versatile shape, Pebbleford is the most widely collected, followed by Dwarf Pine, pastel lines, and decaled lines. (We cover Pebbleford in chapter 10.) The remaining Versatile lines are receiving increased attention by collectors and prices have begun to rise.

When Versatile is found as a partial set it is usually reasonable and makes a good buy for the collector. With patience, missing pieces can be found to complete the service. Collectors will often have to buy items in Dwarf Pine and the pastel lines individually, paying a higher price.

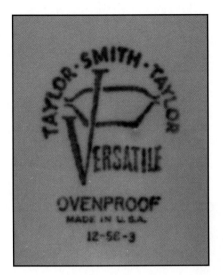

Versatile cups.
From left: casual type from a 1958 set $1.75, formal type from a 1960 set
$1.75, mid 1960s type $1.75, and the original 1952 design $1.75.

Versatile backstamp.
The profile of the casserole was
used as the logo for the shape.

Versatile platter dipped in Lu-Ray's
Persian Cream $4.00.

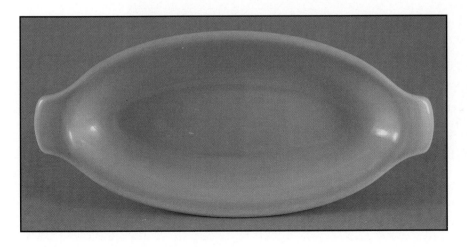

Pickle in Versatile dipped in
Lu-Ray's Surf Green. Late 1950s.
$6.00.

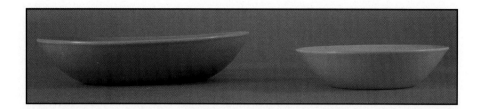

Low profile oval vegetable $3.50, and fruit $1.50, in Lu-Ray colors on Versatile.

Third design for Versatile teacup and saucer, mid 1950s. $3.00.

Versatile plates in an unnamed pastel line. From left: 10" dinner plate $2.00, 9" lunch plate $1.75, 6" bread and butter $1.50. All dated 1958 and 1959.

*Versatile informal line of
chop plate $6.00,
salt and pepper shakers $5.00,
oval vegetable $3.50,
platter $4.00, sauceboat $4.00,
dinner plate $2.00, fruit $11.50,
bread and butter plate in Shasta
Daisy $1.50.*

*Versatile informal "Shasta Daisy"
handled covered sugar $3.25,
cup and saucer $3.00,
cream $2.75.*

*Unknown Versatile line.
Dated 6–62. The sugar bowl is
missing its cover.*

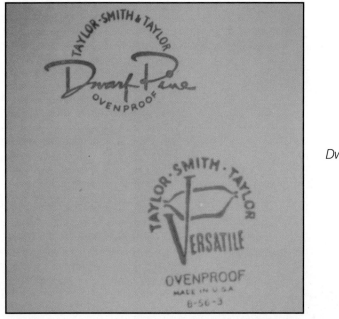

Dwarf Pine backstamps.

After-dinner coffee cup and saucers on the Lu–Ray shape in Dwarf Pine.
Note the two variations of the Dwarf Pine decal on the saucers $17.25.

Dwarf Pine on Versatile
covered sugar and cream $7.00.

*Dwarf Pine decal on Versatile
dinner plate $2.50, fruit $1.75,
coupe soup $2.00, platter $4.50,
cup and saucer $3.50.*

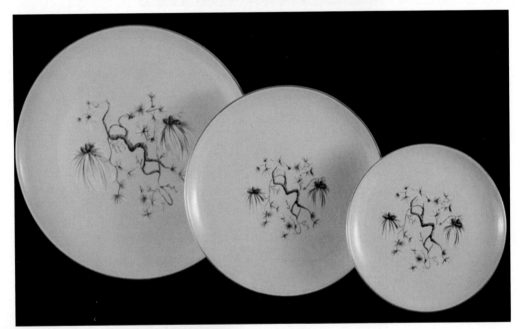

*Dwarf Pine chop plate $7.00, dinner plate
$2.50, salad plate $2.00, all on Versatile.*

*Formal version of the Versatile coffee server
in an unidentified pattern $21.00.*

Versatile platter $4.00,
cup and saucer $3.00,
chop plate $6.00,
salad plate $1.75,
coupe soup $1.75.

Formal type Versatile
cream $2.75,
covered sugar $3.25,
coffee server $21.00,
salt shaker $2.50.

Lug handled toast rack
compatable with Versatile,
Pebbleford, and Ever Yours $3.00.

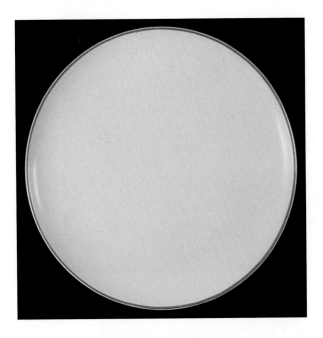

*Simple gilt decoration on a
Versatile shape dinner plate $2.00.*

*Early to mid-1960s
covered sugar and cream $6.00.*

*Early to mid-1960s Versatile in an
unknown pattern. From left:
bread and butter plate $1.50,
cup and saucer $3.00,
dinner plate $2.00,
coupe soup $1.75.*

*"Moulin Rouge" covered casserole on the
Versatile shape $23.00.*

*Unknown decal on Versatile
shape coffee server $21.00.*

CHAPTER 10

PEBBLEFORD,
FOR ROUND-THE-CLOCK MODERN LIVING

1952 to circa 1960

Pebbleford is the best known line on the Versatile shape. Introduced in 1953, Pebbleford best exemplifies Gilkes's concept of an informal, adaptable line. To quote a Pebbleford brochure, the shape was "as Versatile as the day is long."

The Original Pebbleford Line

Pebbleford appeared in a choice of four textured, pastel colors including Sunburst (yellow), Granite (gray), Pink, and Turquoise. The distinctive flecks of russet are actually bits of iron.

The original line consisted of:

Dinner Plate	13" Platter
Salad Plate	Handled Covered Sugar
Bread & Butter Plate	Unhandled Covered Sugar
Fruit	Cream
Lug Soup	Sauceboat
Coupe Soup	Pickle
Coupe Soup (extra large)	Salt
Cup	Pepper
Saucer	Teapot
Vegetable (Round)	Coffee Server
Vegetable (Oval or "medium")	Chop Plate
11" Platter	Covered Casserole

The unhandled sugar bowl is identical to the handled one, except the bottom does not have lugs. It is apparently less common since none could be found to photograph for this book.

The Therma-Role

In January 1954, an interesting accessory piece called the Therma-Role was added to the line. A large, double-walled, covered container in the Versatile shape, it looked much like a covered ice bucket, and was promoted to keep foods either hot or cold. The Therma-Role retailed for $10, while a 16 piece starter set of Pebbleford could then be purchased for only $4.95. Apparently not a big seller, no examples of the Therma-Role have been reported. It does not appear on 1956 price lists and must have been discontinued before then.

TAYLOR, SMITH & TAYLOR: *"Therma-Role,"* one of a number of new accessory pieces added to Pebbleford; double liner keeps food either hot or cold. Retail price, $10.

"The Therma-Role" in Pebbleford. It's double line kept food hot or cold.

Additions To The Line

China, Glass and Decorative Accessories reported in May 1954, that a water jug, egg cup, covered butter dish, and divided vegetable dish or baker had been added to Pebbleford. The egg cup is instantly recognized as the one from the Lu-Ray line, dipped in Pebbleford glazes. The egg cup also disappeared sometime before the 1956 brochures were printed.

The first newly added Pebbleford color was White or Marble White added in January 1956. Later that year, Granite was discontinued, replaced by Mint Green keeping the number of colors at five. Discontinued with Granite were two items that had been offered earlier in 1956 in White. They were the coupe soup (extra large) and the teapot, which was identical in form but shorter than the coffee server. Teal, a dark green must have been introduced sometime in 1956 since egg cups have been found in that color.

Later additions to Pebbleford's color palette were Sand, a creamy pumpkin pie color; Honey, a more beige yellow than Sunburst; and Burnt Orange.

Burnt Orange

Burnt Orange is believed to have been the latest addition, probably dating to 1959 or 1960. Most early Pebbleford pieces have backstamps, often with production dates. Backstamps are limited to dinner plates on later Pebbleford items and often lack dates of manufacture.

"Reveille"

Some decaled lines based on Pebbleford may be found. "Reveille," a rooster decal on Honey Pebbleford, dates to late in the line's production or perhaps shortly after.

Like the Versatile shape on which it is based, the Pebbleford line was meant to be adaptable to any meal setting. "From a casual luncheon to a crystal-and-candlelight dinner, the pleasant, soft colors of Pebbleford create harmonious warmth and cheer."

COLLECTING PEBBLEFORD

In Pebbleford, Sunburst, Pink, and Turquoise are the most common colors, probably because they were the most popular originally and were made during its entire production run. Mint Green, Honey, and Burnt Orange, the last to be added to the line, are the most scarce. So far they are priced the same as the other colors. The textured glazes of Pebbleford complement the abstract, sometimes surreal forms of Versatile especially well, making it a 1950s design classic. These lines were made in some quantity and fragments of sets can still be found, but more often collectors will have to buy individual pieces of Pebbleford.

A collection of saucers displaying Pebbleford's colors. From left: Sunburst, Pink, Turquoise, White, Granite, Teal, and Sand. Not shown: Mint Green, Honey, and Burnt Orange.

Granite Pebbleford cream and handled covered sugar $12.00.

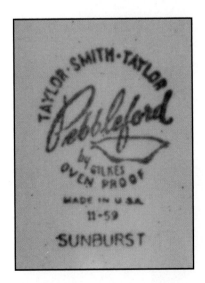

Pebbleford backstamp. Since Pebbleford is on the Versatile shape, its backstamp also uses the profile of the casserole as part of its logo.

Pebbleford in turquoise and yellow.
Clockwise: cup and saucer $5.00, coupe soup $3.00, salad plate $3.00, dinner plate $3.00, fruit $2.00, bread and butter plate $2.50.

Pebbleford bowls in turquoise.
Clockwise: vegetable (oval) $7.00, vegetable (round) $7.00, coupe soup $3.00.

Pebbleford covered casserole on Granite (gray) $30.00.

Pink Pebbleford covered butter $17.00.

Divided baker in Pink Pebbleford $23.00.

Pebbleford covered casserole $30.00, and handled covered sugar in Pink $7.00.

Sunburst Yellow Pebbleford water jug $25.00.

This Pink Pebbleford item may be a syrup pitcher $20.00.

Pebbleford pickle $12.00, lug soup $5.00, round vegetable $7.00, medium vegetable $7.00, all in Sunburst. A lid has been found to fit the lug soup.

Pebbleford serving pieces in Sunburst. From left, backrow: coffee server $25.00, round vegetable $7.00, water jug $25.00, middle row: sauceboat $8.00, pickle $12.00, front row: oval or medium vegetable $7.00.

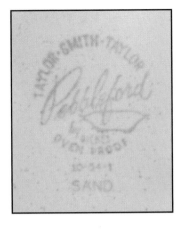

Pebbleford backstamp on
Sand. Dated 10–54.

Sand Pebbleford vegetable bowl $7.00.

Pebbleford salt and pepper shakers in Sand $5.00.

Pebbleford Teal oval vegetable $7.00.

Pebbleford Granite saucer $2.00,
Teal dinner plate $3.00, Sand bread
and butter plate $2.50.

Pebbleford 13" platters in
Pink and Teal $7.00 ea.

Pink Pebbleford
covered casserole $30.00.

*Pebbleford Burnt Orange.
From Left: handled covered
sugar $7.00, cream $5.00,
fruit $2.00,
bread and butter $2.50,
dinner plate $3.00,
coupe soup $3.00,
salad plate $3.00,
round vegetable $7.00,
cup and saucer $5.00.*

*Burnt Orange dinner plate in Pebbleford
$3.00.*

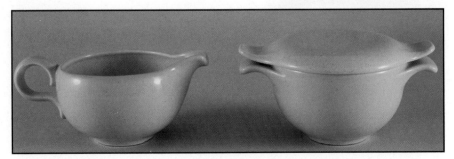

*Pebbleford Sunburst
cream $5.00, covered sugar $7.00.*

Backstamp of "Reveille" line dinner plate. These were not marketed as Pebbleford.

Pebbleford egg cup in the Lu-Ray shape $10.00.

"Reveille" line dinner plate $3.00, 15" platter $7.00.

"Reveille" line on Honey Pebbleford. From left: coupe soup $3.00, covered butter $17.00, chop plate $15.00, cup and saucer $5.00.

10" Calendar plate for 1958 on Pink Pebbleford
$35.00.

10" Pebbleford Calendar plate for 1961 in Sunburst
$35.00.

Unknown green Pebbleford 10" 1960 calendar plate
shown for contrast with mint green
Pebbleford cup $35.00 and saucer $5.00.

Pebbleford coffee server with decorated lid $25.00.
Most coffee servers use a 4" lid. Variations have been
found fitted with a 3" lid.

111

1956 Pebbleford brochure.

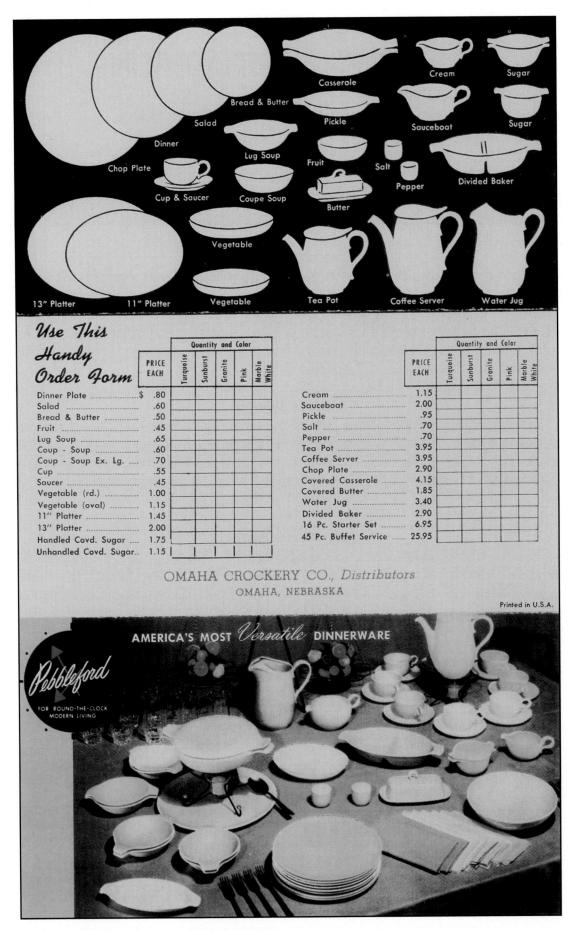

Use This Handy Order Form

Item	PRICE EACH	Turquoise	Sunburst	Granite	Pink	Marble White
Dinner Plate	$ .80					
Salad	.60					
Bread & Butter	.50					
Fruit	.45					
Lug Soup	.65					
Coup - Soup	.60					
Coup - Soup Ex. Lg.	.70					
Cup	.55					
Saucer	.45					
Vegetable (rd.)	1.00					
Vegetable (oval)	1.15					
11" Platter	1.45					
13" Platter	2.00					
Handled Covd. Sugar	1.75					
Unhandled Covd. Sugar	1.15					

Item	PRICE EACH	Turquoise	Sunburst	Granite	Pink	Marble White
Cream	1.15					
Sauceboat	2.00					
Pickle	.95					
Salt	.70					
Pepper	.70					
Tea Pot	3.95					
Coffee Server	3.95					
Chop Plate	2.90					
Covered Casserole	4.15					
Covered Butter	1.85					
Water Jug	3.40					
Divided Baker	2.90					
16 Pc. Starter Set	6.95					
45 Pc. Buffet Service	25.95					

OMAHA CROCKERY CO., *Distributors*
OMAHA, NEBRASKA

Printed in U.S.A.

AMERICA'S MOST *Versatile* DINNERWARE

Pebbleford
FOR ROUND-THE-CLOCK MODERN LIVING

Reverse side of Pebbleford brochure.

CHAPTER 11

IN THE
CONTINENTAL TRADITION

Chateau Buffet and Oven-Serve
1956 to 1965

Chateau Buffet, which is oven-to-table serving ware, was another line created by John Gilkes. Designed for casual entertaining, T.S.&T. sales literature described each piece by its French name in keeping with its continental theme.

The Chateau Buffet Line

Items in the Chateau Buffet line included large, 4½ quart and medium, 2½ quart casseroles ("La Grande Terrine" and "La Terrine Moyenne"), a set of six individual casseroles ("Les Ramequins"), a salad bowl with fork and spoon ("Le Saladier"), and a 10 cup carafe with warmer ("La Carafe"). Cups, saucers, and dinner plates, lacking the French titles of the serving pieces, completed the ensemble. Chateau Buffet was available in Cinnamon and Turquoise.

Timeless Design

"...Old world charm and beauty with a graceful contemporary touch... generous size vessels for entertaining... timeless in design, modern in serviceability... oven and detergent-proof..." stated the copy in the Chateau Buffet brochure. Chateau Buffet met all of Gilkes's criteria for ware to suit the casual American lifestyle.

Oven-Serve Ware

Genuine T.S.&T. Oven-Serve Ware appeared in the early 1960s. This floral-embossed ware in Yellow, Pink, Brown and Turquoise is virtually identical to a ware made by other U.S. potteries. The ware may have been made to the specifications of a customer who ordered it in quantity from a number of potteries. It also may have been given away as a premium.

So far, Oven-Serve ramekins, individual casseroles and custard cups have been found in this line. Pieces are backstamped or marked in the mold. Examples of this line are readily available to today's collectors.

COLLECTING CHATEAU BUFFET

So far, the Chateau Buffet and Oven-Serve lines have few followers and can be had reasonably when they are found. Most pieces can be easily identified by the incised mark on the bottom. Examples of this line are difficult to find in good condition, suggesting it was more often used for daily meals than for occasional entertaining. Many pieces available in the Chateau Buffet line appear to have had hard use and perfect examples are harder to find than in Oven-Serve. Since other American potteries made very similar or identical ware the collector should only buy pieces clearly marked with an incised or ink T.S.&T. backstamp.

Incised mark on Chateau Buffet bowl.

Oven-Serve backstamp on a custard.

Oven-Serve incised in the mold mark.

Chateau Buffet bowl $3.00–5.00.

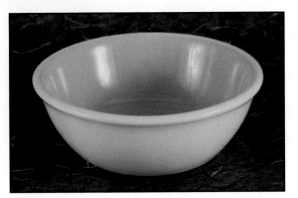

115

Custard cups, casserole, ramekin, in the Oven-Serve line. The average price of these pieces today is $3.00–5.00 except for the casserole, which is difficult to price due to its scarcity.

Oven-Serve ramekins $3.00–5.00, and custard cups $3.00–5.00.

Oven-Serve casserole.

CHAPTER 12

AMERICAN FINE CHINA

Taylorton
1958 to circa 1965

As low cost imports continued to flood the market and plastic dinnerware became increasingly popular, T.S.&T. found its sales figures beginning to fall. The company leaders realized that they had to find a new market niche.

Affordable China

Design director John Gilkes, creator of Versatile and Pebbleford, believed that he had the answer. He set out to establish T.S.&T. as a leader in inexpensive china. Gilkes felt an affordable china could replace T.S.&T.'s staple of semi-vitreous ware and successfully compete with foreign dinnerware and plastics. Gilkes wrote an article which appeared in the July 30, 1959, issue of the *Potters Journal* explaining his concept.

He wrote "To many people, the thought of eating from fine china every day is pretty revolutionary. And there's a good reason. Fine American china used to be expensive... few people will risk the danger of damaging a precious piece. As a result, the china only comes out on Sunday, or for 'company.' Yet the very reasons for owning china are the reasons why it should be used every day... The sense of luxury and well-being from seeing and using fine china is an experience the whole family can enjoy, and should enjoy, every day."

A Harder Glaze

Mr. Gilkes succeeded in developing a line of china called Taylorton and promoted it as "American Fine China." Part of Taylorton's appeal is its glaze. Harder than other American glazes of its time, it resisted knife marks. And, unlike most china, it was oven-proof. As Gilkes explained, the customer didn't "have to buy separate baking dishes for the foods you want to serve hot out of the oven."

Cost Controls

T.S.&T. knew that in order to keep its prices comparable to, or lower than, foreign china, they had to control the cost of making Taylorton. T.S.&T. reduced their labor costs by developing and using automatic machinery as much as possible. To reduce waste resulting from inferior batches of raw materials, Taylorton's clays, feldspar, and flint were blended at the plant to be uniform. The contents of each railroad freight car was quality tested before it was unloaded to be sure it met T.S.&T.'s high standards.

A Distinctive Design

Gilkes wrote that Taylorton's design "had to have a familiar appearance, yet be utterly distinctive. And accessory pieces had to do double duty wherever possible... the design must not offend a sense of order, whether on the dinner table or in the living room. For example, the... sauceboat... is as much at home with nuts, candy, or cheese dip in the living room as it is with gravy or sauce in the dining room."

The design of Taylorton, as with all of Gilkes's creations, was to "look as well for 'dinner-at-eight' or a late buffet supper, as for everyday use... Distinctiveness and grace were supplied by a slight Persian influence in some of the pieces. And, for a touch of greater elegance, ceramic knobs and touches of polished brass were added," wrote Gilkes.

Ironstone Replaces Chinaware

Over time the demand for ironstone gradually increased until it replaced china and semi-vitreous dinnerware. About the time T.S.&T. was sold to Anchor-Hocking the production of chinaware was stopped. While this decision was based partly on the popularity of ironstone, it was also due to T.S.&T.'s realization, after decades of trying, that it could no longer compete with imported china or semi-vitreous ware.

COLLECTING TAYLORTON

Ironically, while Taylorton was T.S.&T.'s finest quality line, it is little collected by dinnerware fans today. That situation is sure to change. Interest in the designs of the late 1950s and early 1960s are increasing and collectors are sure to discover John Gilkes and his work. Taylorton best represents Gilkes's design principles for dinnerware, casual yet elegant, appropriate in any setting, made of the finest quality materials and workmanship but affordable for the average family.

Taylorton still turns up regularly at yard sales and thrift shops, unrecognized. It is usually found in complete services for eight or fragments of sets. The most difficult to find items are serving pieces like coffee servers which were sold separately.

Taylorton backstamp.

Taylorton in the "Dianthus" pattern covered sugar and cream $6.00.

"Candlelight" pattern on Taylorton. Shown are the cereal/soup $1.75, dinner plate $2.00, cup and saucer $3.00, bread and butter plate $1.50.

Taylorton "Echo Dell" backstamp.

"Echo Dell" dessert dish on Taylorton $1.50.

USE THIS HANDY ORDER FORM

	Happy Talk		Ivory Tower			Happy Talk		Ivory Tower	
	No. of Pieces	Price Each	No. of Pieces	Price Each		No. of Pieces	Price Each	No. of Pieces	Price Each
Cup		1.75		1.40	Sauceboat		2.95		2.60
Saucer		1.00		.95	Sauceboat-Util. Tray		2.95		2.80
Bread & Butter Plate		1.10		1.05	Bread Tray		7.95		7.25
Salad Plate		1.60		1.50	Salt & Pepper		3.00 pr.		2.85 pr.
Dinner Plate		2.00		1.90	Pepper Mill		6.95		6.75
Dessert Dish		1.10		1.05	Buffet Salt		1.50		1.45
Cereal-Soup		1.60		1.50	Oil & Vinegar		4.95 pr.		4.75 pr.
Covered Sugar		2.95		2.60	Round Platter—11"		2.95		2.80
Creamer		2.30		1.90	Coffee Server		9.95		8.50
Covered Casserole		9.95		8.50	Relish Tray		3.75		3.35
Med. Vegetable		2.50		2.30	Soup Cup		1.50		1.20
Large Vegetable—Salad		2.95		2.80	Ind. Salt-Ash Tray		1.00		.95
Platter—13"		3.95		3.75	*5-pc. Place Setting		5.95		4.75
16-pc. Starter Set		16.95		13.95	45-pc. Set		44.95		37.95

Name_____

Address_____

City & State_____

☐ Charge   ☐ C.O.D.   ☐ Payment Enclosed

Walnut Warmer 4.95
*incl. Cup, Saucer, 6" and 10" plates and soup

OMAHA CROCKERY CO.
1116 Harney Street   Omaha 2, Nebraska
TST-858-2O   25M   4/59   PRINTED IN U.S.A.

Brochure for the "Happy Talk" pattern on Taylorton. Dated April 1959.

USE THIS HANDY ORDER FORM

	Echo Dell (Blue) No. of Pieces	Echo Dell (Blue) Price Each	Echo Dell (White) No. of Pieces	Echo Dell (White) Price Each		Echo Dell (Blue) No. of Pieces	Echo Dell (Blue) Price Each	Echo Dell (White) No. of Pieces	Echo Dell (White) Price Each
Cup		1.75		1.50	Sauceboat		2.95		2.75
Saucer		1.00		1.00	Sauceboat-Util. Tray		2.95		2.95
Bread & Butter Plate		1.10		1.10	Bread Tray		7.95		7.50
Salad Plate		1.60		1.60	Salt & Pepper		3.00 pr.		3.00 pr.
Dinner Plate		2.00		2.00	Pepper Mill		6.95		6.95
Dessert Dish		1.10		1.10	Buffet Salt		1.50		1.50
Cereal-Soup		1.60		1.60	Oil & Vinegar		4.95 pr.		4.95 pr.
Covered Sugar		2.95		2.75	Round Platter—11"		2.95		2.95
Creamer		2.30		2.00	Coffee Server		9.95		8.95
Covered Casserole		9.95		8.95	Relish Tray		3.75		3.50
Med. Vegetable		2.50		2.50	Soup Cup		1.50		1.25
Large Vegetable—Salad		2.95		2.95	Ind. Salt-Ash Tray		1.00		1.00
Platter—13"		3.95		3.95	*5-pc. Place Setting		5.95		4.95
16-pc. Starter Set		16.95		14.95	45-pc. Set		44.95		39.95

Name_____

Address_____

City & State_____

☐ Charge   ☐ C.O.D.   ☐ Payment Enclosed

*incl. Cup, Saucer, 6" and 10" plates and soup

OMAHA CROCKERY CO.

1116 Harney Street   Omaha 2, Nebraska

TST-460-118 40M 4/60 PRINTED IN U.S.A.

Taylorton AMERICAN FINE CHINA . . . AT A PRICE YOU CAN AFFORD!

ECHO DELL (BLUE)
Also available with white holloware interiors

A John Gilkes Design

Taylorton Fine China brochure dated April 1960. The pattern shown is "Echo Dell" (blue).

Taylorton Fine China brochure dated April 1960.

CHAPTER 13

EVER YOURS

1958 to circa 1965

The Ever Yours shape inherited its flatware pieces and informal style from Versatile. Like Gilkes's original concept for Versatile, it was meant for casual, everyday meals in or out of the dining room.

Gilkes designed imaginative hollowware pieces to complete the new line. Abstract, almost free-form in appearance, its coffee server resembles a saxophone. Produced alongside the more formal Classic shape, Ever Yours was phased out around 1965.

COLLECTING EVER YOURS

Some of John Gilkes's most interesting designs for T.S.&T. are on the Ever Yours shape. While solid-colored wares have always been favored by collectors, Gilkes imaginitive, Space Age shapes coupled with the often subtle patterns of the period will make these standout favorites with the next generation of collectors. For now, these lines, less common than Laurel or Empire, can still be found in partial or complete sets. Serving pieces, other than bowls, platters, creams, and sugars, require more searching by collectors but the many unusual items make it worth the effort. All are still reasonably priced.

Ever Yours cake server $15.00, carafe $12.50, and warming stand $5.00. The cork lined walnut stopper is probably a Timbercraft product made by T.S.&T. The brass finial on the stopper and stand were purchased from a supplier.

Boutonniere line on the Ever Yours shape. Dinner plate $2.00, cup and saucer $3.00, salad plate $1.75.

Boutonniere on Versatile shape lug soup $3.00.

Sauce boat (with underliner) with Boutonniere decal on Ever Yours $6.50.

Salt & pepper shakers $5.75,
and covered butter $5.75,
in Boutonniere on the
Ever Yours shape.

Cups on Ever Yours.
Left: Boutonniere $1.75,
right: Twilight Time $1.50.
(Note variations in handles.)

Ever Yours shape
Twilight Time backstamp.

Twlight Time on the Ever Yours shape.
Shown here are the dinner plate $1.75,
coupe soup $1.50, salad plate $1.50,
cup and saucer $2.50, dessert dish $1.25.

Ever Yours utility tray $8.00, and covered casserole $18.00 in Twilight Time.

Ever Yours Boutonniere backstamp.

Ever Yours casserole lined in Blue. Probably used with Boutonniere and other lines $18.00.

Rooster line backstamp. Rooster is thought to be based on the Ever Yours shape.

Cape Cod line water jug $15.00.

*Rooster on an unknown shape.
Salad plate $1.50,
coupe soup $1.50,
dessert dish $1.25.*

*Harmony House backstamp,
made to special order by T.S.&T.*

*Ever Yours cups.
Left: Weathervane line $1.50,
right: Mocha Pine $1.50,
(for Harmony House).*

Mocha Pine dinner plate on the Ever Yours shape $1.75 (for Harmony House).

Ever Yours dinner plate in the Woodrose line $1.75.

"Peppermint Roc" 15" platter in colorcraft line $3.00. Colorcraft is believed to be based on Ever Yours.

Summertime line on Ever Yours cake plate $6.00 While this plate is part of the Ever Yours shape, it is "pick up piece" recycled from the Laurel shape.

Autumn Harvest dinner plate on the Ever Yours shape $1.75.

Ever Yours carafe in the Autumn Harvest pattern $12.50.

Ever Yours cake server in the Autumn Harvest pattern $15.00.

Autumn Harvest covered butter $5.00, tea tile $20.00, salt and pepper shakers $5.00, on the Ever Yours shape

129

CHAPTER 14

CLASSIC

1960 to 1972

> To appeal to the market for formal dinnerware, Gilkes created the Classic shape around 1960. Gilkes combined a new design for simple flatware with a generous flange and the same formal hollowware he created for Versatile in 1955. The result is a traditional, but not stodgy, timeless ware.

Two-Toned Patterns

Many patterns appeared on this shape during the 1960s. Most patterns on this shape are two-toned, a color on the flange with a white center on the flat pieces. Many patterns are decorated with a gold or platinum trim.

Classic was the last semi-vitreous shape developed by T.S.&T. Over time it was overshadowed by ironstone. It was discontinued when T.S.&T. eliminated all but ironstone lines from production in 1972.

COLLECTING CLASSIC

In the Classic shape, the simple, undecaled lines are the most popular with collectors. Not yet discovered by most American dinnerware collectors, some collectors of European dinnerware have pronounced it the most sophisticated American dinnerware design. There is something quintessentially American about its simple form and generously-sized cups and dinner plates. As with Taylorton and Ever Yours, it is still inexpensive and most items are not too hard to find.

Classic backstamp.

Heritage Green Classic backstamp.

*Moon Landing commemorative plate
on Heritage Green Classic $5.00.*

*Platinum Blue on the Classic shape
backstamp.*

*Bread and butter plate $2.50, cup and saucer $5.00
in Platinum Blue on the Classic shape.*

*A strong family resemblance exists
between the formal type of
Versatile cup $1.75, and
the Platinum Blue cup $3.00,
on the Classic shape.*

CHAPTER 15

IRONSTONE

Taylorstone, Taylor Ironstone, and Related Lines
1963 to 1981

By 1963 T.S.&T. had developed its first ironstone line, Taylorstone. It was designed by John Gilkes. The plates resemble the Classic semi-vitreous ware shape while the hollowware alternates between low-profile pieces, like the covered casserole, and tall, cylindrical items, like the coffee server and the cream.

Taylor Ironstone Patterns

Taylorstone was followed by Design 70 (and Granada) from about 1967 to 1975, and Taylor Ironstone from about 1970 to 1975. Some T.S.&T. ironstone lines were marked simply "ironstone" along with the name of the line and manufacturer.

Taylor Ironstone was offered in many patterns including Aztec, Buttercup, Champagne, Flower Tree, Gingham Garden, Indian Morn, Lilac Wreath, Love Song, Mountain Meadow, Morning Glory, Petit Bouquet, Pink Posie, Plaid, Sierra, Springdale, Springtime, Yellow Gingham, Williamsburg Wheat, and Wood Rose. Ultimately, the popularity of ironstone and T.S.&T.'s inability to compete with imported china and semi-vitreous ware would cause all but ironstone to be dropped from production.

COLLECTING IRONSTONE

T.S.&T.'s final generation of products, Taylorstone, Taylor Ironstone, etc. are just becoming collectible. Many of these lines are still plentiful in thrift shops and Goodwill stores. Again, so many patterns were made in these lines we have not seen examples of all of them. The earliest lines, Taylorstone and Taylor Ironstone, as well as the later Design 70 and Granada lines, are the most desireable.

Taylorton Designs Autumn Bouquet backstamp.

*Taylorton Designs Autumn Bouquet
dinner plate $1.50.*

*Taylorton Ironstone Flora line, dinner plate $1.50.
Circa 1970.*

*Taylor Ironstone
Flora line backstamp.*

*Kristina line on Taylorstone
dinner plate $1.50. Mid-late 1960s.*

Matador on the Granada shape
Ironstone backstamp.

Cathay line on Classic shape
Taylorstone dinner plate $1.50. Mid-1960s.

Matador divided vegetable $6.00, round vegetable $3.50, and cereal/soup $1.75,
on the Granada Ironstone shape.

*Design 70 backstamp,
Indian Summer line.*

*Matador line ironstone on the Granada shape, mid to late 1960s.
Clockwise: platter $4.00, salad plate $1.75,
cup and saucer $3.00, dinner plate $2.00.*

*Design 70 covered butter $5.00,
and sauceboat $4.00, faststand in
the Indian Summer line.*

*Taylorstone Sirocco
line backstamp.*

*Sirocco salad plate
on Taylorstone $1.25.*

Yorkshire Brown line
Taylor Ironstone backstamp.

Taylor Ironstone Yorkshire Brown
dinner plate $1.25, circa 1970.

Wood Flower on Taylor Ironstone covered sugar $2.00, cup and saucer $1.50,
dinner plate $1.25, cereal/soup $1.00, bread and butter plate .75¢, cream $1.75.
These date to the early 1970s.

CHAPTER 16

THE CERAMICS PRODUCTS DIVISION OF ANCHOR HOCKING CORPORATION

1972 to 1981

> As T.S.&T. entered the 1970s it met ever increasing competition from imported dinnerware. Despite the best efforts of the company to modernize and automate to control labor costs, it was difficult to contend with the lower labor costs of foreign manufacturers, especially those in Asia.

T.S.&T. Sold to Anchor Hocking

In 1972 the stockholders voted to allow T.S.&T. to be bought by glass-making giant Anchor Hocking of Lancaster, Ohio. In a 1983 interview with the *Potters Herald*, William A. Foley, Consumer & Industrial Division Vice President, mentioned that Anchor Hocking felt its ability to offer glassware along with dinnerware would give it a major advantage over competitors. The combined firm could coordinate glassware and dinnerware patterns in low-cost ensembles.

T.S.&T., now the Ceramic Products Division of Anchor Hocking Corp., would benefit from the parent company's huge sales force and regional distribution centers. Most T.S.&T. employees were retained or transferred to other Anchor Hocking plants.

Unfortunately, T.S.&T. under Anchor Hocking was ultimately unsuccessful. Their products were still unable to compete with the low price of imported dinnerware. Some smaller potteries were able to move faster in designing and marketing new dinnerware patterns. Sales slowly declined until, in 1981, Anchor Hocking decided to discontinue dinnerware production.

The Closing of the Chester, West Virginia, Plant

Anchor Hocking discussed selling T.S.&T. to the Lenox China Company, makers of high quality china, "but the plant in general did not meet the specifications of their company" reported the *Potters Herald*. Unable to find a buyer for T.S.&T., Anchor Hocking announced it would close the Chester, West Virginia, plant by December 31,1981. The pottery, which once employed almost 700 workers, then employed about 400. Some employees were transferred to other Anchor Hocking operations and those who were eligible were permitted to retire. The rest were laid off.

One newly installed kiln and manufacturing line were removed from the pottery and placed in another Anchor Hocking plant in Lancaster, Ohio. The remaining equipment and contents of the dinnerware plant were sold at auction. Items considered to have no value, like left-over sales brochures, were destroyed. The plant and its adjacent properties were then sold.

A Plant Stands Empty

Since T.S.&T.'s closing, nostalgia for modern dinnerware influenced the Homer Laughlin China Company to put its Fiesta line back into production. Imported dinnerware lines in Lu-Ray's lovely colors are offered in department and kitchen specialty stores, begging the question, would Lu-Ray be a viable product today?

The former T.S.&T. plant is still empty. A beauty parlor occupies the pottery's engineers' building. The art department building, once a house, is a private home again. The house occupied by the advertising department has been torn down and an apartment building has been built on part of the employees' parking lot.

Lucky Stones

Today, the giant plant, once bustling with the activity of 700 workers, is quiet. Nearby, at the edge of the river, in the shadow of the pottery dump, children laugh and play as they search for "lucky stones." Most do not realize the "lucky stones," polished smooth by the flow of the river, are fragments of the pottery made by their grandparents and great-grandparents.

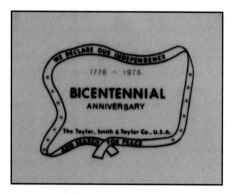

Backstamp on a Bicentennial plate.

Bicentennial plate $8.00.
Most of these had an applied Liberty Bell in the center.

Taylor mug.
These were sold in sets $1.00.

Incised mark.
Taylor International on a Taylor mug.

Taylor Mugs, dating to the late 1960s – early 1970s $1.00 each.

VALUE GUIDE

Prices were derived from a sampling of items recently offered for sale by dealers coast to coast. Any prices that appeared to be unusually low or high were eliminated from the sample. These suggested values should only be used as a guide. Prices will vary in different parts of the country.

Items we have designated "very rare" are too few in number to provide a reasonable idea of their value.

Lu-Ray Pastels

ITEM	FOUR COLORS	GRAY
Teacup	$7.00–10.00	$15.00–18.00
Tea Saucer	$2.00–3.00	$5.00–6.00
Plate, 6"	$3.00–5.00	$10.00–13.00
Plate, 7"	$8.00–12.00	$12.00-18.00
Plate, 8"	$12.00-18.00	$20.00-26.00
Plate, 9"	$8.00–12.00	$14.00–20.00
Plate, 10"	$13.00–18.00	$17.00–25.00
Coupe Soup "flat"	$10.00–15.00	$18.00-25.00
Lug Soup "tab"	$15.00–22.00	$25.00–35.00
Fruit, 5"	$4.00–6.00	$10.00–15.00
Fruit, 6½"	Very Rare	*
Dish, "Platter," 7"	Very Rare	*
Dish, "Platter," 11½"	$11.00–15.00	$18.00-25.00
Dish, "Platter," 13"	$13.00–18.00	$20.00-28.00
Nappy, "Round Vegetable," 8½"	$10.00–15.00	$20.00–25.00
Baker, "Oval Vegetable," 9½"	$13.00–18.00	$22.00–30.00
Sauceboat, "Gravy"	$12.00-15.00	*
Pickle, "Celery or Utility"	$20.00–28.00	*
Sugar, Covered	$10.00–12.00	$25.00–35.00
Cream	$6.00–10.00	$20.00–30.00
Casserole	$60.00–80.00	*
Teapot "flat spout"	$60.00–75.00	*
Teapot "curved spout"	$45.00–65.00	Very Rare
Salt Shaker	$5.00–8.00	$12.00–15.00
Pepper Shaker	$5.00–8.00	$12.00–15.00
Chop Plate, 15"	$20.00–30.00	Very Rare
Water Jug "footed"	$50.00–70.00	*
Water Jug "Pitcher"	$40.00–60.00	*
Cream Soup Cup "Bowl"	$48.00–60.00	*
Cream Soup Saucer	$20.00–25.00	*

ITEM	FOUR COLORS	GRAY
Sauceboat, Fixed Stand	$18.00–25.00	$25.00–35.00
Cake Plate	$55.00–75.00	*
Relish Dish	$65.00–95.00	*
Flower Vase "Epergne"	$90.00–125.00	*
Double Egg Cup	$12.00–18.00	$22.00–28.00
Bowl, 36's "Oatmeal Bowl"	$25.00–40.00	*
Bud Vase	$200.00–225.00	*
Bud Urn "Urn Vase"	$200.00–225.00	*
After-Dinner Coffee Pot	125.00–150.00	*
After-Dinner Coffee Pot "Chocolate Pot"	$350.00–375.00	*
After-Dinner Coffee Cup	$15.00–22.00	$28.00–35.00
After-Dinner Coffee Cup "Chocolate Pot Set"	$50.00–70.00	*
After-Dinner Coffee Saucer	$7.00–10.00	$8.00–10.00
After-Dinner Coffee Saucer "Chocolate Pot Set"	$20.00–25.00	*
After-Dinner Individual Covered Sugar	$35.00–45.00	*
After-Dinner Individual Covered Sugar "Chocolate Pot Set"	$85.00–100.00	*
After-Dinner Individual Cream	$35.00–45.00	*
After-Dinner Individual Cream "Chocolate Pot Set"	$85.00–100.00	*
Muffin Cover	$65.00–80.00	*
Compartment Plate "Grill"	$18.00–25.00	$60.00–85.00
Fruit Juice Jug "Pitcher"	$100.00–130.00	*
Fruit Juice Tumbler	$30.00–40.00	*
Salad Bowl	$38.00–55.00	*
Covered Butter	$35.00–40.00	$80.00–100.00
Bowl 10¼"	$75.00–100.00	*
Bowl, 8¾"	$70.00–90.00	*
Bowl, 7"	$70.00–90.00	*
Bowl, 5½"	$75.00–100.00	*
Tumbler	$45.00–65.00	*
Coaster "Nut Dish"	$60.00–75.00	*
Calendar Plates, 8", 9" & 10"	$35.00–50.00	*

* Item not produced in gray according to T.S.&T. brochures.

Items noted as "Very Rare," while they do not appear listed in Lu-Ray Pastels brochures, price lists, or advertising, backstamped examples are known to exist.

Early Shapes - 1900 to 1935

The earliest items by T.S.&T., those with the griffin backstamp and most lines of the 1910s and 1920s, are very scarce. We were unable to find enough examples to price them accurately, except to suggest their values would be comparable to other dinnerware of the period. The same is true of the institutional Chester Hotel China.

For the late 1920s–early 1930s Paramount shape, values are suggested as follows:

Paramount

Teacup	$5.00
Tea Saucer	$2.50
Plate, 6"	$3.00
Plate, 7"	$4.00
Plate, 10"	$5.00
Soup Bowl	$7.00
Fruit	$3.00
Platter	$10.00
Nappy "Round Vegetable"	$6.00
Baker "Oval Vegetable"	$10.00
Sauceboat	$8.00
Pickle	$7.00
Sugar, Covered	$6.00
Cream	$5.00
Casserole	$30.00
Teapot	$50.00
Batter Jug, Covered	$40.00
Syrup Jug, Covered	$30.00

There may be more items on the Paramount shape than listed here. For the Avona and Iona shapes, add 20% to the above list.

1930 to 1955

Vogue, Delphian, Beverly, Fairway, Garland, and Plymouth		Castle, Center Bouquet, Delphian Rose, Dogwood, and English Abbey*	
Teacup	$2.50	Teacup	$5.00
Tea Saucer	$2.00	Tea Saucer	$3.50
Plate, 6"	$2.25	Plate, 6"	$6.00
Plate, 7"	$2.50	Plate, 7"	$8.00
Plate, 9"	$2.00	Plate, 9"	$10.00
Plate, 10"	$3.00	Plate, 10"	$12.50
Soup Bowl	$2.50	Soup Bowl	$12.50
Fruit	$2.00	Fruit	$5.00
Small Platter	$6.50	Small Platter	$20.00
Large Platter	$8.00	Large Platter	$30.00
Nappy "Round Vegetable"	$3.50	Nappy "Round Vegetable"	$15.00
Baker "Oval Vegetable"	$5.50	Baker "Oval Vegetable"	$15.00
Sauceboat	$7.50	Sauceboat	$18.00
Cake Plate	$10.00	Cake Plate	$20.00
Pickle	$7.00	Pickle	$10.00
Sugar, Covered	$5.50	Sugar, Covered	$12.00
Cream	$3.50	Cream	$10.00
Casserole	$27.00	Casserole	$35.00
Teapot	$25.00	Teapot	$50.00

Use "Castle," "Center Bouquet," etc. values to price "Mexican Fantasy."

*The "Castle," "Center Bouquet,""Delphian Rose," "Dogwood," and "English Abbey" patterns are prized more highly than the average pattern. Resembling nineteenth century English transferware, they are bought by many collectors of antique pottery as well as American dinnerware enthusiasts. English Abbey backstamps do not mention T.S.&T. and may have been a special order given away as premiums.

Pastoral, 1950s

Teacup	$3.00
Tea Saucer	$2.00
Bread & Butter Plate	$2.50
Fruit	$2.50
Cereal Bowl	$3.50

	Laurel and Empire	Silhouette or Taverne
Teacup	$2.00	$10.00
Tea Saucers	$1.50	$2.00
Plate, 6"	$1.75	$5.00
Plate, 7"	$2.00	$15.00
Plate, 8"	$9.00	$20.00
Plate, 9"	$2.00	$10.00
Plate, 10"	$2.50	$25.00
Coupe Soup "flat"	$2.00	$15.00
Lug Soup "tab"	$4.00	$25.00
Fruit	$1.50	$7.00
Dish, "Platter," 7"	$7.00	$20.00
Dish, "Platter," 11½"	$5.00	$25.00
Dish, "Platter," 13"	$6.00	$30.00
Nappy, "Round Vegetable"	$4.00	$25.00
Baker, "Oval Vegetable"	$6.00	$30.00
Sauceboat	$7.00	
Cake Plate	$10.00	
Pickle	$7.00	
Sugar, Covered	$5.00	$20.00
Cream	$4.00	$15.00
Casserole	$25.00	$75.00
Teapot (flat spout)	$25.00	*
Teapot (curved spout)	$20.00	*
Salt Shaker	$4.00	**
Pepper Shaker	$4.00	**
Cake Plate	$9.00	*
Bowl, 36's	$10.00	$40.00
Covered Butter	$10.00	$150.00
St. Denis Cup	***	$35.00
St. Denis Saucer	***	$7.00

* No examples of these items were found.

** Salt and pepper shakers in this line are believed to have been made by Hall China Company.

*** St. Denis cups have not been found with a T.S.&T. backstamp and have not been found with any other T.S.&T. line. However, since the St. Denis saucers have appeared marked T.S.&T. both are believed to be T.S.&T. products.

NOTE: Patterns which resemble English Staffordshire ware, such as "Center Bouquet," "Castle," "Dogwood," etc. can command a premium. They are sometimes sold and collected as a "poor man's" substitute for these early 19th century English patterns. Collectors of English Staffordshire pottery might pay four to five times the values for the 1930s lines.

Vistosa
1938 to circa 1942

Teacup	$10.00–15.00
Tea Saucer	$5.00–7.00
Plate, 10"	$50.00–60.00
Plate, 9"	$15.00–20.00
Plate, 7"	$12.00–18.00
Plate, 6"	$10.00–15.00
Coupe Soup	$20.00–25.00
Lug Handled Soup	$25.00–30.00
Fruit	$10.00–15.00
Nappy	$40.00–50.00
Chop Plate, 12"	$30.00–40.00
Chop Plate, 15"	$40.00–50.00
Covered Sugar	$20.00–25.00
Cream	$15.00–20.00
Teapot, 6 cup	$80.00–100.00
Footed Salad Bowl, 12"	$175.00–200.00
Water Jug, 2 quart	$75.00–85.00
Salt Shaker	$10.00–15.00
Pepper Shaker	$10.00–15.00
Footed Egg Cup	$25.00–30.00
After-Dinner Coffee Cup	$30.00–35.00
After-Dinner Coffee Saucer	$15.00–20.00
Sauceboat	$100.00–125.00

Coral-Craft
1939

Pricing Coral-Craft is difficult as few pieces are available. Some collectors value it above Lu-Ray while others have little interest in the line. Our limited experience suggests prices plus or minus 20% those for Lu-Ray Pastels.

Conversation
1950–1954

Dinner Plate	$2.50
Salad Plate	$2.00
Bread & Butter Plate	$1.75
Fruit	$1.50
Soup	$2.00
Cup	$2.00
Saucers	$1.50
Vegetable (round)	$3.00
Vegetable (small oval)	$5.00
Vegetable (large oval)	$6.00
Platter	$5.00
Covered Sugar	$5.00
Cream	$3.00
Sauceboat	$7.00
Coffee Server	$20.00
Covered Casserole	$25.00
Covered Butter	$9.00
Water Jug	$25.00
Salt & Pepper Shakers	$5.00

Add 15% for items in the "King O' Dell" pattern.

Versatile
1952 – circa 1965

Dinner Plate	$2.00
Lunch Plate	$1.75
Salad Plate	$1.75
Bread & Butter Plate	$1.50
Fruit	$1.50
Lug Soup	$2.50
Coupe Soup	$1.75
Coupe Soup, extra large	*
Cup	$1.75
Saucer	$1.25
Vegetable (round)	$2.25
Vegetable (oval)	$3.50
11" Platter	$3.00
13" Platter	$4.00
Handled Covered Sugar	$3.25
Unhandled Covered Sugar	*
Cream	$2.75
Sauceboat	$4.00
Pickle	$6.00
Salt	$2.50
Pepper	$2.50
Teapot	$20.00
Coffee Server	$21.00
Chop Plate	$6.00
Covered Casserole	$23.00
Covered Butter	$5.50
Water Jug	$15.00
Divided Baker	$15.00
After-Dinner Coffee Cup	$12.00
After-Dinner Coffee Saucer	$3.00
Therma-Role	*
Double Egg Cup	$10.00

* No examples of these items were found.
Add 15% when pricing "Dwarf Pine."

Pebbleford
1952 – circa 1960

Dinner Plate	$3.00
Salad Plate	$3.00
Bread & Butter Plate	$2.50
Fruit	$2.00
Lug Soup	$5.00
Coupe Soup	$3.00
Coupe Soup extra large	*
Cup	$3.00
Saucers	$2.00
Vegetable (small round)	$6.00
Vegetable (large round)	$7.00
Vegetable, medium (oval)	$7.00
11" Platter	$6.00
13" Platter	$7.00
Handled Covered Sugar	$7.00
Unhandled Covered Sugar	*
Cream	$5.00
Sauceboat	$8.00
Pickle	$12.00
Salt	$2.50
Pepper	$2.50
Teapot	$20.00
Coffee Server	$25.00
Chop Plate	$15.00
Covered Casserole	$30.00
Covered Butter	$17.00
Water Jug	$25.00
Divided Baker	$23.00
Therma-Role	*
Double Egg Cup	$10.00
Calendar Plates	$35.00

* No examples of these items were found.

Chateau Buffet and Oven-Serve
1956 – circa 1965

Small items in the Chateau Buffet line can be had for an average of $3.00–$5.00 each. Larger pieces such as the carafe and casserole are difficult to find and to price. Oven Serve items can be had for an average $3.00 to $5.00 each.

Taylorton
1958 – circa 1965

Cup	$1.75
Saucer	$1.25
Bread & Butter Plate	$1.50
Salad Plate	$1.75
Dinner Plate	$2.00
Dessert Dish	$1.50
Cereal/Soup	$1.75
Covered Sugar	$3.25
Creamer	$2.75
Covered Casserole	$23.00
Medium Vegetable	$2.25
Large Vegetable/Salad	$3.50
Platter	$4.00
Sauceboat	$4.00
Sauceboat/Utility Tray	*
Bread Tray	*
Salt & Pepper	$5.00
Pepper Mill	*
Buffet Salt	*
Oil & Vinegar	*
Round Platter, 11"	$6.00
Coffee Server	$21.00
Relish Tray	*
Soup Cup	*
Individual Salt/Ashtray	*

* No examples of these items were found.

Ever Yours
1958–1965

Cup	$1.50
Saucer	$1.00
Bread & Butter Plate	$1.25
Salad Plate	$1.50
Dinner Plate	$1.75
Dessert Dish	$1.25
Lug Soup	$2.50
Coupe Soup	$1.50
Covered Sugar	$3.00
Creamer	$2.50
Covered Casserole	$18.00
Vegetable (round)	$3.00
Covered Vegetable	$15.00
Platter (oval)	$3.00
Sauceboat (with underliner)	$5.50
Utility Tray	$8.00
Round Platter	$6.00
Salt & Pepper	$5.00
Coffee Server	$20.00
Water Jug	$15.00
Covered Butter	$5.00
Cake Plate	$6.00
Carafe	$12.50
Cake Server	$15.00
Tea Tile	$20.00
Warming Stand	$5.00

Add 15% when pricing Boutonniere.
Use Ever Yours values to price the Colorcraft, Harmony House, and Rooster lines.

Classic
1960–1970

Use the values for Taylorstone when pricing items on the Classic shape. Use the values for Pebbleford for pieces in Platinum Blue.

Taylorstone
1963–1981

Cup	$1.25
Saucer	$ .75
Bread & Butter Plate	$1.00
Salad Plate	$1.25
Dinner Plate	$1.50
Dessert Dish	$1.00
Cereal/Soup	$1.25
Covered Sugar	$2.50
Creamer	$2.00
Covered Casserole	$10.00
Vegetable	$1.75
Platter	$2.75
Sauceboat	$3.25
Covered Butter	$3.75
Coffee Server	$10.00

Use Taylorstone values to price the Design 70 and Granada shape lines.

Taylor Ironstone and other Ironstone lines

Cup	$1.00
Saucer	$ .50
Bread & Butter Plate	$ .75
Salad Plate	$1.00
Dinner Plate	$1.25
Dessert Dish	$ .75
Cereal/Soup	$1.00
Covered Sugar	$2.00
Creamer	$1.75
Covered Casserole	$8.00
Vegetable	$1.50
Platter	$2.50
Sauceboat	$3.00
Covered Butter	$3.50
Coffee Server	$8.00

Use the Taylor Ironstone for pricing all other late T.S.&T. ironstone lines not covered elsewhere.

The Ceramic Products Division Of Anchor Hocking Corporation

Taylor Mug $1.00
Bicentennial Plate $8.00

BIBLIOGRAPHY

Beautiful Caverns of Luray The, Luray Caverns Corp., Luray, VA, n.d.

Brochures, Lu-Ray Pastels, The Taylor, Smith & Taylor Company, n.d.

China, Glass & Tableware, Clifton, NJ 1930-1981.

Crockery and Glass Journal, 1930–1955.

Cunningham, Jo. *The Collector's Encyclopedia of American Dinnerware*, Collector Books, Paducah, KY 1982.

Current Biography, *Who's News and Why*, 1942. Maxine Block, ed. The H.W. Wilson Co., New York, NY 1942

Duke, Harvey. *Official Identification and Price Guide to Pottery and Porcelain*, 7th ed. Ballantine Books, New York, NY 1989.

Encyclopedia of World Art, Vol. I. McGraw-Hill Book Co., n.d.

Evening Review The, article "Ceramic Sesquicentennial," East Liverpool, OH, April 29, 1989.

Heide, Robert and John Gilman. *Popular Art Deco*. Abbeville Press, New York, NY 1991.

Huxford, Sharon & Bob. *The Collector's Encyclopedia of Fiesta*, 7th ed. Collector Books, Paducah, KY 1992.

Kerr, Ann. *The Collector's Encyclopedia of Russel Wright*. Collector Books, Paducah, KY 1990.

Kovel, Ralph & Terry. *Kovel's Depression Glass & American Dinnerware Price List*, 3rd Edition, Crown Publishers, Inc., New York, NY 1988.

Ledes, Allison Eckhardt. *The Magazine Antiques*, February, 1994 "Commercial Design" in the "Current and Coming" section.

Potters Herald, Vol. LXXIX No. 6, October 1981.

Sterling Book, Listing the Products of The Taylor, Smith & Taylor Company, East Liverpool, OH, 1942.

Whitmyer, Margaret & Kenn. *The Collector's Encyclopedia of Hall China*. Collector Books, Paducah, KY, 1989.

If you have information about Lu-Ray Pastels or other T.S.&T. lines, please write to us. Maybe we will be able to include what you have found in the future editions of this book.

Bill & Kathy Meehan
P.O. Box 2054
Haddonfield, NJ 08033

Books on Antiques and Collectibles

This is only a partial listing of the books on antiques that are available from Collector Books. All books are well illustrated and contain current values. Most of the following books are available from your local book seller, antique dealer, or public library. If you are unable to locate certain titles in your area, you may order by mail from COLLECTOR BOOKS, P.O. Box 3009, Paducah, KY 42002-3009. Customers with Visa or MasterCard may phone in orders from 8:00 – 4:00 CST, M – F – Toll Free 1-800-626-5420. Add $2.00 for postage for the first book ordered and $0.30 for each additional book. Include item number, title, and price when ordering. Allow 14 to 21 days for delivery.

BOOKS ON GLASS AND POTTERY

1810	American Art Glass, Shuman	$29.95
1312	Blue & White Stoneware, McNerney	$9.95
1959	Blue Willow, 2nd Ed., Gaston	$14.95
3719	Coll. Glassware from the 40's, 50's, 60's, 2nd Ed., Florence	$19.95
3816	Collectible Vernon Kilns, Nelson	$24.95
3311	Collecting Yellow Ware – Id. & Value Gd., McAllister	$16.95
1373	Collector's Ency. of American Dinnerware, Cunningham	$24.95
3815	Coll. Ency. of Blue Ridge Dinnerware, Newbound	$19.95
2272	Collector's Ency. of California Pottery, Chipman	$24.95
3811	Collector's Ency. of Colorado Pottery, Carlton	$24.95
3312	Collector's Ency. of Children's Dishes, Whitmyer	$19.95
2133	Collector's Ency. of Cookie Jars, Roerig	$24.95
3723	Coll. Ency. of Cookie Jars-Volume II, Roerig	$24.95
3724	Collector's Ency. of Depression Glass, 11th Ed., Florence	$19.95
2209	Collector's Ency. of Fiesta, 7th Ed., Huxford	$19.95
1439	Collector's Ency. of Flow Blue China, Gaston	$19.95
3812	Coll. Ency. of Flow Blue China, 2nd Ed., Gaston	$24.95
3813	Collector's Ency. of Hall China, 2nd Ed., Whitmyer	$24.95
2334	Collector's Ency. of Majolica Pottery, Katz-Marks	$19.95
1358	Collector's Ency. of McCoy Pottery, Huxford	$19.95
3313	Collector's Ency. of Niloak, Gifford	$19.95
3837	Collector's Ency. of Nippon Porcelain I, Van Patten	$24.95
2089	Collector's Ency. of Nippon Porcelain II, Van Patten	$24.95
1665	Collector's Ency. of Nippon Porcelain III, Van Patten	$24.95
1447	Collector's Ency. of Noritake, 1st Series, Van Patten	$19.95
1034	Collector's Ency. of Roseville Pottery, Huxford	$19.95
1035	Collector's Ency. of Roseville Pottery, 2nd Ed., Huxford	$19.95
3314	Collector's Ency. of Van Briggle Art Pottery, Sasicki	$24.95
3433	Collector's Guide To Harker Pottery - U.S.A., Colbert	$17.95
2339	Collector's Guide to Shawnee Pottery, Vanderbilt	$19.95
1425	Cookie Jars, Westfall	$9.95
3440	Cookie Jars, Book II, Westfall	$19.95
2275	Czechoslovakian Glass & Collectibles, Barta	$16.95
3882	Elegant Glassware of the Depression Era, 6th Ed., Florence	$19.95
3725	Fostoria - Pressed, Blown & Hand Molded Shapes, Kerr	$24.95
3883	Fostoria Stemware - The Crystal for America, Long	$24.95
3886	Kitchen Glassware of the Depression Years, 5th Ed., Florence	$19.95
3889	Pocket Guide to Depression Glass, 9th Ed., Florence	$9.95
3825	Puritan Pottery, Morris	$24.95
1670	Red Wing Collectibles, DePasquale	$9.95
1440	Red Wing Stoneware, DePasquale	$9.95
1958	So. Potteries Blue Ridge Dinnerware, 3rd Ed., Newbound	$14.95
3739	Standard Carnival Glass, 4th Ed., Edwards	$24.95
3327	Watt Pottery – Identification & Value Guide, Morris	$19.95
2224	World of Salt Shakers, 2nd Ed., Lechner	$24.95

BOOKS ON DOLLS & TOYS

2079	Barbie Fashion, Vol. 1, 1959-1967, Eames	$24.95
3310	Black Dolls – 1820 - 1991 – Id. & Value Guide, Perkins	$17.95
3810	Chatty Cathy Dolls, Lewis	$15.95
1529	Collector's Ency. of Barbie Dolls, DeWein	$19.95
2338	Collector's Ency. of Disneyana, Longest & Stern	$24.95
3727	Coll. Guide to Ideal Dolls, Izen	$18.95
3822	Madame Alexander Price Guide #19, Smith	$9.95
3732	Matchbox Toys, 1948 to 1993, Johnson	$18.95

3733	Modern Collector's Dolls, 6th series, Smith	$24.95
1540	Modern Toys, 1930 - 1980, Baker	$19.95
3824	Patricia Smith's Doll Values – Antique to Modern, 10th ed	$12.95
3826	Story of Barbie, Westenhouser, No Values	$19.95
2028	Toys, Antique & Collectible, Longest	$14.95
1808	Wonder of Barbie, Manos	$9.95
1430	World of Barbie Dolls, Manos	$9.95

OTHER COLLECTIBLES

1457	American Oak Furniture, McNerney	$9.95
3716	American Oak Furniture, Book II, McNerney	$12.95
2333	Antique & Collectible Marbles, 3rd Ed., Grist	$9.95
1748	Antique Purses, Holiner	$19.95
1426	Arrowheads & Projectile Points, Hothem	$7.95
1278	Art Nouveau & Art Deco Jewelry, Baker	$9.95
1714	Black Collectibles, Gibbs	$19.95
1128	Bottle Pricing Guide, 3rd Ed., Cleveland	$7.95
3717	Christmas Collectibles, 2nd Ed., Whitmyer	$24.95
1752	Christmas Ornaments, Johnston	$19.95
3718	Collectible Aluminum, Grist	$16.95
2132	Collector's Ency. of American Furniture, Vol. I, Swedberg	$24.95
2271	Collector's Ency. of American Furniture, Vol. II, Swedberg	$24.95
3720	Coll. Ency. of American Furniture, Vol III, Swedberg	$24.95
3722	Coll. Ency. of Compacts, Carryalls & Face Powder Boxes, Mueller	$24.95
2018	Collector's Ency. of Granite Ware, Greguire	$24.95
3430	Coll. Ency. of Granite Ware, Book 2, Greguire	$24.95
1441	Collector's Guide to Post Cards, Wood	$9.95
2276	Decoys, Kangas	$24.95
1629	Doorstops – Id. & Values, Bertoia	$9.95
1716	Fifty Years of Fashion Jewelry, Baker	$19.95
3817	Flea Market Trader, 9th Ed., Huxford	$12.95
3731	Florence's Standard Baseball Card Price Gd., 6th Ed.	$9.95
3819	General Store Collectibles, Wilson	$24.95
3436	Grist's Big Book of Marbles, Everett Grist	$19.95
2278	Grist's Machine Made & Contemporary Marbles	$9.95
1424	Hatpins & Hatpin Holders, Baker	$9.95
3884	Huxford's Collectible Advertising – Id. & Value Gd., 2nd Ed	$24.95
3820	Huxford's Old Book Value Guide, 6th Ed.	$19.95
3821	Huxford's Paperback Value Guide	$19.95
1181	100 Years of Collectible Jewelry, Baker	$9.95
2216	Kitchen Antiques – 1790 - 1940, McNerney	$14.95
3887	Modern Guns – Id. & Val. Gd., 10th Ed., Quertermous	$12.95
3734	Pocket Guide to Handguns, Quertermous	$9.95
3735	Pocket Guide to Rifles, Quertermous	$9.95
3736	Pocket Guide to Shotguns, Quertermous	$9.95
2026	Railroad Collectibles, 4th Ed., Baker	$14.95
1632	Salt & Pepper Shakers, Guarnaccia	$9.95
1888	Salt & Pepper Shakers II, Guarnaccia	$14.95
2220	Salt & Pepper Shakers III, Guarnaccia	$14.95
3443	Salt & Pepper Shakers IV, Guarnaccia	$18.95
3890	Schroeder's Antiques Price Guide, 13th Ed.	$12.95
2096	Silverplated Flatware, 4th Ed., Hagan	$14.95
2348	20th Century Fashionable Plastic Jewelry, Baker	$19.95
3828	Value Guide to Advertising Memorabilia, Summers	$18.95
3830	Vintage Vanity Bags & Purses, Gerson	$24.95

Schroeder's
ANTIQUES
Price Guide

. . . is the #1 best-selling antiques & collectibles value guide on the market today, and here's why . . .

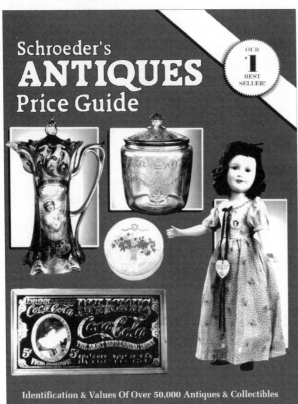

Schroeder's ANTIQUES Price Guide

OUR #1 BEST SELLER!

Identification & Values Of Over 50,000 Antiques & Collectibles

8½ x 11, 608 Pages, $12.95

• *More than 300 advisors, well-known dealers, and top-notch collectors work together with our editors to bring you accurate information regarding pricing and identification.*

• *More than 45,000 items in almost 500 categories are listed along with hundreds of sharp original photos that illustrate not only the rare and unusual, but the common, popular collectibles as well.*

• *Each large close-up shot shows important details clearly. Every subject is represented with histories and background information, a feature not found in any of our competitors' publications.*

• *Our editors keep abreast of newly developing trends, often adding several new categories a year as the need arises.*

If it merits the interest of today's collector, you'll find it in *Schroeder's*. And you can feel confident that the information we publish is up to date and accurate. Our advisors thoroughly check each category to spot inconsistencies, listings that may not be entirely reflective of market dealings, and lines too vague to be of merit. Only the best of the lot remains for publication.

Without doubt, you'll find
SCHROEDER'S ANTIQUES PRICE GUIDE
the only one to buy for
reliable information and values.

COLLECTOR BOOKS
A Division of Schroeder Publishing Co., Inc.